WORLD WAR II
HEROES

WORLD WAR II HEROES

By Allan Zullo

SCHOLASTIC INC.

No part of this publication may be reproduced, stored in a retrieval system, or transmitted in any form or by any means, electronic, mechanical, photocopying, recording, or otherwise, without written permission of the publisher. For information regarding permission, write to Scholastic Inc., Attention: Permissions Department, 557 Broadway, New York, NY 10012.

ISBN 978-0-545-81841-4

12 11 10 9 8 7 6 5 4   16 17 18 19 20/0

Printed in the U.S.A.   40
First Scholastic printing, July 2015

To Mike Gorospe, everyone's friend
and Sasha's hero
—AZ

Contents

The War and Its Heroes   1

"We've Got to Fight Back!"
Chief Petty Officer John Finn   5

The Stowaway
Private First Class Jack Lucas   18

American Bushido
Lieutenant Richard Antrim   32

Attack in the Devil's Sea
Commander Lawson "Red" Ramage   47

Hero Without a Gun
Private First Class Desmond Doss   61

Flying Blind
Sergeant Forrest "Woody" Vosler   74

Mission Impossible
Lieutenant Colonel James Rudder   90

The Ghost
Captain Matt Urban   105

From Jerk to Hero
Sergeant Maynard "Snuffy" Smith   118

Buffalo Soldier
Second Lieutenant Vernon Baker   132

WORLD WAR II
HEROES

The War and Its Heroes

Powerful, ruthless countries rolled out their fearsome war machines in the 1940s in a fanatical attempt to rule the world. It was up to the defenders of freedom to stop them. Answering the call, courageous soldiers, sailors, airmen, and marines willingly sacrificed life and limb to preserve liberty for tens of millions of people around the globe in the most horrific war in history.

World War II started after Germany, led by dictator Adolf Hitler and the Nazi Party, invaded Poland in 1939. This caused Great Britian and France, which were allies of Poland, to declare war on Germany. Nazi forces then invaded and occupied Denmark, Norway, Belgium, Holland, Luxembourg, France, Yugoslavia, and Greece. Italy teamed up with Germany, and together they battled British forces in North Africa. By the summer of 1941, Germany had conquered most of Western Europe and then attacked the Soviet Union. For nearly six years, the Nazis battered Great Britain with devastating air assaults night after night, but the Germans underestimated the headstrong resolve of the British, who put up a steely resistance.

For two years, the United States stayed out of the war, although it sent a steady stream of vital supplies to Great Britain.

Meanwhile, on the other side of the world, Japan, which had invaded China in 1937, was trying to conquer East and Southeast Asia, despite protests from the United States. On December 7, 1941, Japan launched surprise attacks against several countries, as well as the American naval base at Pearl Harbor, Hawaii.

The United States had no choice but to declare war on Japan, Germany, and Italy — the three major countries that formed an alliance called the Axis Powers. America joined the Allied Powers, which was made up of dozens of nations that opposed the Axis Powers. The Allies were spearheaded by the United States, Great Britain, the Soviet Union, Australia, and Canada.

The American military — Army, Army Air Corps (now known as the Air Force), Navy, Marines, and Coast Guard — were forced to fight German and Italian forces in Europe as well as the Japanese throughout the South Pacific.

After devastating early setbacks, the Allies rallied and began winning raging battles in Europe and successfully invaded Italy in 1943. On June 6, 1944 — forever known as D-day — the Allies launched the world's greatest invasion, at Normandy in France. Less than a year later, they drove the Germans out of Western

Europe, liberating all the once-conquered countries. Germany finally surrendered on May 8, 1945.

In the South Pacific region, the Japanese scored major victories early in the war, but then Allied forces fought back with a vengeance. American submarines blocked supplies of oil and raw materials to Japan, and Allied invasions of key islands, such as Iwo Jima and Okinawa, further crippled the Japanese. On August 15, 1945 — just days after the United States dropped the first atomic bombs on the Japanese cities of Hiroshima and Nagasaki — the Empire of Japan surrendered.

World War II, which involved more than 70 nations, resulted in the deaths of an estimated 60 million people, making it the deadliest conflict in recorded history. The men and women in the U.S. military paid a dear price for victory: 406,000 killed; another 671,000 seriously wounded.

Those fighting for our country were everyday citizens who felt duty bound to protect and preserve the values that made America great. An untold number of them found deep within themselves incredible courage they didn't know they had. In firefights in the bombed-out fields of France, in dogfights over the flak-filled skies of Belgium, in hand-to-hand combat on the bloody beaches of Okinawa, Americans discovered an intense bravery that spurred them to reach far beyond their personal limits.

They became the valiant heroes of World War II.

You are about to read the gripping stories of 10 of them. These accounts are based on memoirs, battle reports, and military files. Using real names, dates, and places, the stories are written as factual versions of their heroism, although certain scenes have been dramatized and some dialogue has been re-created. For realism, the dialogue contains a few words referring to the Japanese and German soldiers that by today's standards are considered offensive but were commonly used in the heat of combat back then.

Most of the heroes featured in this book earned the Medal of Honor — our country's highest award for valor in combat above and beyond the call of duty. Of the 16 million Americans who served in World War II, only 440 were awarded the medal, including 250 who received it after they had died.

These 10 stories spotlight soldiers, sailors, airmen, and marines who stared the enemy — and death — in the face and still managed to carry out their missions. They were among the ones who performed heroic deeds despite their fears. They were the ones who succeeded against overwhelming odds. They were the ones who helped win the war and save the world.

"We've Got to Fight Back!"

CHIEF PETTY OFFICER
JOHN FINN

When John Finn woke up on a bright Sunday morning, December 7, 1941, he planned a relaxing day off with his wife, Alice, in their palm-tree-shaded bungalow on the Hawaiian island of Oahu.

By the time he went to bed the next night, his life and the world he once knew had changed forever.

Chief Petty Officer Finn was in charge of ammunition at a small naval air station nestled on a cove at Kaneohe Bay a mile from his house. The little base was the home of 36 twin-engine seaplanes known as PBYs that were anchored in the water, tied down on a parking ramp, or sheltered in one of three hangars. At the time, the United States was not at war with anyone. But because Japan was becoming a growing threat, the men at the air station were on limited alert. They flew routine patrols looking for Japanese submarines off the coast and checking on nearby Pearl Harbor, where several Navy destroyers, battleships, and other vessels were moored.

"Wake up, honey," Finn cooed to Alice. "It's almost eight o'clock and it's another beautiful day in paradise."

Alice pulled the covers over her head and mumbled, "You start the coffee, and then I'll get up."

As Finn padded barefoot into the kitchen, he heard the sounds of machine-gunfire in the distance in the direction of the base. *It's Sunday morning. Why would anyone be firing machine guns at the range today?* he wondered. Finn filled the pot with water and spooned in the coffee. Then he heard the whines of small planes. They weren't the usual rumbling sounds of the PBYs. *Maybe some wise-guy aviators are buzzing the barracks.* He looked out the window and didn't see anything unusual. But he sensed that something wasn't right.

Finn returned to the bedroom and put on his white Navy uniform shirt, pants, hat, and black shoes. "Honey, I'm going to the station for just a few minutes, and then I'll be right back." He kissed Alice, walked out, and hopped into his 1938 Ford.

On the way toward Kaneohe, Finn, a 15-year veteran who had joined the Navy when he was only 17, thought about how far he had come from those troubled teenage days back home in Compton, California. *I have a great wife, I live in Hawaii, and I'm making decent money. Not bad for a high-school dropout.*

A loud roar from above interrupted his thoughts. Peering out of his open car window, he spotted a silver plane flying low and fast. When it banked, he saw a red ball painted on the underside of the wing. It could mean only one thing — it was a

Zero, a fast single-engine fighter-bomber with the Japanese insignia on it.

"Oh, no!" he shouted. "The Japs are attacking us!"

He floored the accelerator and sped toward the air station. On the way, he heard the screaming of more Zeros, dozens upon dozens of them heading west. *They're going to bomb Pearl Harbor!*

When his Ford squealed around the last curve before the air station, he stared in disbelief. Like angry hornets, Zeros were dive-bombing the airfield as one explosion after another erupted into orange balls of fire. The planes' machine guns were raking the parked PBYs while panic-stricken sailors were running helter-skelter in confusion and fear, ducking behind anything that provided cover. The unlucky ones were being mowed down by strafing or were already sprawled on the ground dead or dying. Smoke was billowing up from scores of fires. *My God, all hell is breaking loose!*

Finn's car screeched to a stop near the seaplanes' parking ramp, and he made a mad dash for one of the hangars. During his sprint, a Zero skimming only 100 feet off the ground fired several rounds that kicked up dirt just inches from Finn's feet. He rushed into the hangar as bullets pelted the metal siding. Inside, several men were crouched under desks.

"The war is on!" Finn bellowed. "The Japs are here!"

One of the sailors muttered, "I didn't know they were *that* sore at us."

"Come on!" Finn yelled. "We've got to fight back!"

"With what?" countered another sailor. "We don't have any antiaircraft guns."

"We'll fight 'em with whatever we've got. Our country is being attacked, so we must shoot back. Let's go!"

He led the small group to the armory next door, flung open the back of an ordnance truck that was parked inside, and passed out machine guns and ammunition. "Just start shooting at those Zeros, and let 'em know we're not taking this lying down."

When Finn emptied the truck of weapons, he told the rest of the men to yank out the .50-caliber and .30-caliber machine guns in the PBYs. In the fiery, explosive chaos outside, men darted into the burning wreckages and retrieved ammo and any guns that weren't damaged. Then they began firing at the Japanese planes.

How dare those Japs attack us! Finn thought. *How dare they think they can sweep over our island and bomb our planes and ships without any resistance. Well, we'll show 'em!*

Filled with a fury he had never felt before, Finn picked up a .30-caliber machine gun, which weighed more than 30 pounds, and ran outside and began firing it in the sky. "No one attacks America and gets away with it!" he shouted. But without having a tripod to rest the heavy weapon on, the slightly built five-foot nine-inch Finn found it almost impossible to shoot with any accuracy.

This probably isn't the smartest thing to do, but we need to retaliate. Finn realized that to be effective, he needed a bigger weapon. He charged back into the burning armory and hauled out a .50-caliber machine gun, which weighed more than 80 pounds, and set it on a tripod on an instruction platform in the open by the parking ramp. His only cover was from the billowing smoke of the nearby hangar that was burning out of control. But he didn't care. He had no fear — only rage. *I'm going to shoot 'em down until they shoot me off this platform.*

Armed with several lengthy belts of ammunition, he began firing back at the Zeros as they continued their deadly bombing and strafing runs. Explosions still rocked the air station and bullets tore into the PBYs on the field and in the water, causing several of them to burst into flames.

The loud *rat-a-tat-tat* fire from his machine gun drowned out the shrieking and whining of the swooping Zeros. Not for a second did Finn think of his own safety — not even when bullets from the planes slammed into the platform. *They have to pay a price for this! They have to know that they can't get away with a surprise attack without losing their own lives!*

Every time he saw the painted red ball — the Japanese symbol for the rising sun — under the wings of the Zeros, he seethed with anger and vowed to use it as a bull's-eye. When he used up one ammo belt, he swiftly loaded another into the machine gun and kept up his fire as the enemy roared overhead.

Because he was out in the open and harassing the Japanese, Finn could no longer be ignored by the enemy. While he was focused on trying to knock down a Zero coming in from the left, he failed to notice that another plane zooming in on his right was taking aim directly at him.

Bullets ripped into the platform, sending sharp bits of wood and metal ripping into his legs. Finn stopped shooting and dropped to his knees in pain. Seeing blood start to seep through his pants, he looked up at the sky and hollered, "Now you've really ticked me off!" He took a few deep breaths, stood back up, and continued firing at the enemy.

A different Zero on a strafing run peppered the parking area. Once again, Finn was struck, this time in the upper left arm and right thumb. "Ahh! Damn!" He let go of the trigger and looked at his wounds. He noticed that the bullet had gone through a fleshy part of his bicep and, although it hurt, he told himself, *It's no big deal.*

He ignored his bloody thumb and returned his focus to shooting. The barrel of his machine gun was getting red-hot. Low on ammo, he jumped off the platform and limped into the smoke-filled armory where he lugged more heavy belts of ammo. On his way back to the platform, he spotted sailors helping wounded comrades to safety. He saw men firing at low-flying Zeros with rifles and even pistols in a defiant defense of the air station. A sense of pride surged through his wounded body. *We Americans are tough.*

Hobbling past a group of sailors who were firing from behind a truck, he yelled, "We won't give up. We'll never give up!"

The men cheered. One of them then said, "Hey, Finn, you're not going back out there, are you?"

"Yep. That's my post."

Just then a bullet slammed into his thigh, and he tumbled to the ground.

"How badly are you hurt, Finn?"

"It's nothing," he grunted. "The bullet went straight through. It's only a flesh wound." He gathered his ammo belts and limped back to the platform where he loaded his weapon and began shooting again. Just when he had a Zero in his sights, the gun jammed. *Can my luck get any worse?* As he feverishly worked to fix the weapon, a bomb exploded a few yards away, sending small pieces of shrapnel flying into his belly. He fell backward from the impact, leaving him woozy.

His once-crisp white shirt and pants were now covered with blood. After making a quick assessment of his latest injury, he told himself, *I'm hurt, but it doesn't seem to be that serious. Time to get back on my feet. I've got Zeros to shoot down.*

Finn pulled himself up and worked on the machine gun until it was operating again. He had no way of knowing how many planes he hit or damaged or destroyed. All he knew was that he would never quit shooting.

During a brief lull, he felt the pain from his wounds growing in intensity. One of the sailors came over to him and said, "Finn, you're a bloody mess. I'll get you a medic."

"Don't worry about me," Finn said, trying hard not to wince. "It looks worse than it is. Just keep manning your guns. Now, get back to your post!"

Moments later, Finn spotted a Zero far in the distance. It grew larger as it headed directly toward him. *Here's my chance.* The plane dropped lower and kept on its straight-ahead course through a black cloud of smoke at the far end of the air station.

As the Zero emerged from the smoke, Finn saw its propeller churn the smoke in a wispy circle that reminded him of a holiday wreath that his wife, Alice, had hung on the front door the day before. The plane came in lower and looked like it was aiming straight down Finn's gun barrel. Then he saw bursts of light flashing from its wings, its deadly bullets striking the ground in a pattern that tracked right toward him.

Wait, wait, don't shoot too soon, he told himself. Finn's sweaty, bleeding fingers gripped the trigger. The plane was so close now that he could see the pilot's face. *He's grinning at me! The Jap is grinning at me! Not for long!*

Finn squeezed the trigger and fired off several rounds as the plane roared just a few feet over his head. Finn swiveled his machine gun around and shot more bullets at the rear of the Zero. Suddenly, it started spewing smoke from its left wing. The engine coughed, sputtered, and burst into flames. The plane banked sharply to the left and plunged into the woods. Seconds later, Finn heard an explosion and saw smoke rising over the trees.

"I got him!" Finn yelled. "I got him!"

He jumped up in exultation and promptly collapsed on the platform in agony. He looked down at his right shoe, or what was left of it. One of the Zero's bullets had struck Finn's foot. He hadn't noticed the pain while he was shooting at the plane, but he did now. This wound hurt more than the others.

"Finn," yelled a medic who was tending to a wounded sailor about 20 yards away. "Let me help you!"

"Stay where you are," he ordered. "You take care of the others first. I've been scratched up, that's all." He was more than scratched. Finn had bullet holes in his arm and thigh, and shrapnel wounds in his legs, stomach, and chest. He was losing blood. But he wasn't ready to give up; he wasn't willing to abandon his post.

So what if he was badly wounded? It was important to him

to keep fighting back. *No matter what, those Japs can't go unpunished — not by me, my comrades, or my country.*

And so Finn continued to fire his machine gun at every passing Zero. The more he shot, the more he caught the attention of the enemy. Soon every strafing run included gunfire directed at the tough-as-nails chief petty officer. He just kept on shooting. Again and again, he got grazed by a bullet or struck by shrapnel, but he never wavered except for those times when he was brought to his knees momentarily after getting hit. But every time, he rose and continued to man his machine gun.

More than once, fellow Navy men begged him to leave his post and seek medical help, but he waved them off. "I'm not ready yet," he yelled at them. "I've got more Zeros to shoot down."

Finally, after nearly two hours of fighting, the Zeros left almost as quickly as they had come. When the last plane had flown off, the air station fell into an eerie silence except for the crackling of the fires. Finn scanned the skies, wondering if another wave of Japanese planes was on its way. But when he looked around, he knew there was no need for another attack. The Zeros had accomplished their mission. They had virtually destroyed the air station.

Where the hangars once stood, there were only twisted, charred ruins. Every PBY lay bullet-ridden and crumpled, unable to fly. Flames licked out of the broken windows of barracks and other buildings. Men quietly extinguished fires while others carted the wounded and dead off the field, which was littered with wreckage and debris.

Tears welled up in Finn's eyes. He wished he had done more. He wished he and his men had shot down every Zero. He wished the air station had bigger and better weapons to defend itself.

Blood oozed out of his arms, legs, feet, hands, chest, belly, and forehead. He hobbled off the platform, weak and in terrible pain. Trickling out of his heart was the anger that had sustained him throughout the vicious air strike, that had propped him up despite his many wounds. *I need to keep my head clear. I need to start organizing a defense in case the Zeros return.*

"Finn," said a superior officer. "You need help. You're in bad shape."

"So is our air station. I'll see the medics later. But first, we've got a lot of work to do here to prepare for the next possible attack. We need to bring some semblance of order back to Kaneohe Bay." He believed his men needed his experience and leadership now more than ever.

Finn moved slowly because it hurt too much to move at all. With every step, he cringed from his throbbing foot. With every breath, he flinched from the stinging pain in his chest. He ignored the startled expressions of his comrades who were seeing his bloody uniform for the first time.

"I order you to sick bay," the officer told him. "Now!"

Reluctantly, Finn went to a medic but refused to lie down on a cot. "Just patch me up, and I'll come back later for further treatment," Finn said.

"You need to be hospitalized," the medic insisted.

Finn glared at him. "There's too much I have to do. You should be caring for the men who are in worse shape than me. Put some bandages on me to stop the bleeding and let me out of here."

Soon, Finn left to direct men in repairing defenses and setting up machine-gun pits around the air station. Most of these weapons were designed for use on the PBYs, so he had to figure out new ways to mount them on the ground. It was tedious work that went long into the night. Time and again, fellow sailors urged him to seek more treatment for his wounds, but Finn brushed them off. "Not until the work is done," he said.

Eventually, a superior officer approached him and said, "You have gone above and beyond the call of duty. Now it's time to take care of yourself. Get to the sick bay."

"But, sir . . ."

"No 'buts,' Finn. That's an order."

When he staggered into the infirmary, Finn looked at the clock and was stunned at the time. It was 2 A.M. Monday morning. He had been going nonstop for more than 18 hours, fueled in large part by his sense of duty to his fellow men and his country.

Despite the late hour, the sick bay was still bustling as medics scurried around, tending to dozens of seriously wounded men. *No sense waiting around here for a doctor. I need to go home and check on Alice.*

He shuffled outside and looked for his car. *What are the chances that it wasn't damaged? Probably slim to none.* When he reached the back of a bombed-out building, he grinned for the first time since the attack. There was his '38 Ford without a scratch.

Fatigue had set in, and the pain grew worse as he drove home, which, to his relief, wasn't damaged. When he lurched through the front door, Alice shrieked — first out of joy that her husband was alive and then out of shock when she saw he was seriously injured. She ripped off his bloody clothes and tended to the shrapnel cuts and bullet holes on his battered body.

"Dear Lord," she said. "I've counted twenty-one wounds on you. I need to get you to the doctor immediately."

"Later in the morning," he mumbled. "I'm too tired and too hurt to move."

Finn was hospitalized for nearly three weeks. During his stay, he was told terrible news: Twenty people, all but two of them sailors and friends of his, had been killed in the attack at Kaneohe. They were later buried at the air station.

Kaneohe was the first target of the Japanese on that fateful day. Six Japanese aircraft carriers had launched 366 planes in two waves toward Pearl Harbor. At 7:53 A.M., the first bombs fell at Kaneohe. While the air station was being attacked, most of the Zeros went on and struck Pearl Harbor five minutes later, sinking five battleships in only 20 minutes. The *Arizona* met her fate when a bomb hit her magazine, killing 1,177 sailors. Torpedoes and bombs sank the *Oklahoma*, *California*, and *West Virginia* while the *Nevada* grounded herself, trying to escape. Nearly 200 American aircraft were destroyed on the ground. The death toll for Americans soared to 2,330, including 34 pairs of brothers on the *Arizona* alone. The Japanese lost only 64 men, 29 aircraft, and five midget submarines. The next day, the United States declared war on Japan and its ally Germany.

When Finn returned home on Christmas Eve, he told Alice, "The world will never be the same again."

Nine months later, Finn, who had been promoted to lieutenant, was brought aboard the aircraft carrier USS *Enterprise*, which was docked at Pearl Harbor. With the crew and Alice watching, Admiral Chester W. Nimitz awarded Finn the Medal of Honor for extraordinary heroism. After presenting Finn the medal, the admiral said, "Congratulations, Lieutenant. You have made America proud."

Finn blushed and said, "Thank you, sir. I'm just a good old Navy man who was doing his job."

John Finn served on three ships during World War II. He retired from the Navy in 1956 and settled with his wife, Alice, on their cattle ranch in Pine Valley, California. Over the years, buildings at naval installations have been named after him because of his heroism. He celebrated his ninety-seventh birthday on July 23, 2006, knowing he was the oldest living Medal of Honor recipient and the last surviving medal recipient of the Pearl Harbor attack.

The Stowaway

PRIVATE FIRST CLASS
JACK LUCAS

"**Y**esterday, December 7, 1941 — a date which will live in infamy — the United States of America was suddenly and deliberately attacked by naval and air forces of the Empire of Japan."

Thirteen-year-old military school cadet Jack Lucas put his ear closer to the radio as he listened to President Franklin Delano Roosevelt address a stunned nation.

"The attack yesterday on the Hawaiian Islands has caused severe damage to American naval and military forces. Very many American lives have been lost. . . ."

The initial fear that had jangled Jack's nerves began transforming into rage. *The Japs can't do this to us,* he told himself. *We've got to stop them before they invade every town in America. I wish I were older, so I could go into combat and kill them!*

Sitting in his barracks and hearing the president, Jack felt the fury churning inside his gut. It didn't take much to set him off. He had been mad at the world ever since his tobacco-farming father died of cancer two years earlier. Rebellious and angry, the fireplug of a kid with the hair-trigger temper had gone looking for fights and found plenty. He became too much for his widowed mother to handle. That's why he was now wearing the uniform of the Edwards Military Institute in Salemburg, North Carolina.

"Hostilities exist," President Roosevelt continued on the radio. "There is no blinking at the fact that our people, our territory, and our interests are in grave danger. With confidence in our armed forces — with the unbounding determination of our people — we will gain the inevitable triumph — so help us God."

Filled with a fiery blend of patriotism and revenge, Jack pounded his fist into his palm and pledged to himself, *I'm going to join the Marines.*

Of course, he was much too young. The minimum age for military service was 17. But he wasn't about to let an age barrier stop him. Throughout the next year, he badgered his mother to lie about his age so he could enlist, but she refused. The war had intensified in Europe against Nazi Germany and in the Pacific against Imperial Japan. For Jack, not a day went by that he didn't dream of exacting revenge from the Japanese.

There has to be a way I can convince Mama. He had tried

reason. He had tried begging. And then it dawned on him. *I'll threaten to flunk out of military school if she won't let me go.* After he completed eighth grade, Jack issued his ultimatum. Knowing how headstrong he was, his mother reluctantly agreed not to stand in his way if he promised to return to school after the war. He gave her his word.

He forged his mother's consent on enlistment papers that claimed he was 17 and walked into the Marine recruiting office in Norfolk, Virginia. Because he was a muscular five feet eight inches and 165 pounds, he looked much older, so it wasn't that hard for the cocky 14-year-old to talk his way into becoming the newest recruit for the U.S. Marine Corps.

Thanks to his military-school background and his hunger for combat, Jack sailed through basic training and finished at the top of his class in advanced infantry training at Camp Geiger, North Carolina. He had never felt so proud. *I'm a member of the world's greatest fighting force. Now for sure, I'm on my way to fight the Japs.*

When the newly trained Marines were given their individual orders, he ripped open his sealed envelope with happy anticipation. *No, this can't be!* He read it and then read it again. Jack was so good at operating machine guns that he had been ordered to serve as an instructor. *I did not enlist in the Marines to train others. I enlisted to kill the enemy . . . and that's what I'm going to do.*

Lying to his comrades about his orders, he packed his duffel bag and traveled with his unit to Camp Elliott, near San Diego, California, a staging area for Marines heading to combat in the Pacific. Although technically he was AWOL — absent without leave — he wasn't worried. *What's the worst they can do to me? Throw me in the brig for a week or two? Why would they punish me when my sole purpose is to fight the Japs?*

When Jack arrived at Camp Elliott, he convincingly lied to officials that his name had mistakenly been left off the roster, so his was added. He brimmed with excitement. *I'm getting closer to combat.*

On a weekend pass, he had a Marine Corps emblem tattooed on his right bicep. It hurt, but it was a good hurt, because now and forever his body sported the Corps' motto *Semper Fi* (shortened Latin for "always faithful"). *Let me at those Japs!*

At the end of 1943, Jack and his battalion arrived at Camp Catlin in Oahu, Hawaii, where troops prepared to head off to war. So far Private First Class Jack Lucas had fooled everyone. *I'm cranked up and ready to fight. I can't wait.*

But then he made a crucial mistake. He was unaware that all letters sent from camp were read by military censors (people who check mail and delete any information they deem a risk to national security). Jack had written to his sweetheart in Swan Corner, North Carolina, and mentioned "how proud I am to be a Marine, and I'm only fifteen." His cover blown, he found himself standing at attention in front of a stern-faced colonel.

"We are preparing to discharge you from the Marines, Private Lucas."

"Please, sir, don't do that."

"You're too young for the Marines."

"If you try to send me home, sir, I'll simply join the Army and let them benefit from all my training in the Marines."

The colonel leaned back in his chair and sighed. "You win,

Lucas. You can stay in the Marines, but you're not going into combat, not at your age."

Given the job of driving a garbage truck on the base, Jack fumed. *I'm so close to fighting the enemy, I can't give up now.* He pondered every possible angle until he latched onto a plan. It wasn't all that good, actually, but it was the best he could come up with. He noticed that Marines who were troublemakers were usually shipped out to combat right away. *I have to be such a headache for my superiors that they'll send me into action just to get me out of their hair.* So every chance he got, Jack started a fight — 17 brawls in all. And every time, he was locked up in the brig.

Unfortunately, instead of being shipped out, he was sentenced to 45 days of hard labor, pounding rocks 12 hours a day. Another fight, another sentence: this time 30 days on bread and water. Five days after his release, another scrape with the military police cost him 45 more days working the rock pile.

After 18 months at Camp Catlin, Jack finally admitted to himself that his hothead plan wasn't working. He needed to try something else. *I made it this far on bluffs and lies and stowing away on a troop train. Hey, why not stow away again?* In January 1945, Jack, in fatigues and boots, boarded the USS *Deuel*, a Marine troop ship bound for Pacific combat. He didn't care exactly where, just as long as he could fight the enemy that he had sworn to kill.

In an incredible stroke of luck, he found on board his cousin Sam Lucas, a member of the Fifth Marine Division. After the initial shock of seeing Jack, Sam pledged to help him. Getting into the chow line was not a problem, but sleeping arrangements were. Because Jack had no assigned bunk, he secretly slept in one of the launch boats stored on deck.

Sam warned him that after 30 days of AWOL, Jack would be considered a deserter, which in a time of war could mean, if convicted, a sentence of life in prison or even death. "Deserter?" Jack wailed. "How could they think that? Everything I've done — the lies, the fights, the stowing away — has been so I could fight for my country."

Jack waited until the twenty-ninth day at sea before he turned himself in to Lieutenant Colonel Dan Pollock. After hearing his story, Pollock told Jack, "Young fella, you're causing me a whole lot of administrative trouble, but I sure wish I had a whole boatload of men who want to fight as badly as you do. You'll get your wish to fight."

To Jack's joy, he was officially assigned to Company C, First Battalion, Twenty-sixth Marines, his cousin's outfit. When the *Deuel* reached the western Pacific island of Saipan, a Marine who had suffered an appendicitis attack was taken ashore, and Jack was issued the man's rifle and gear.

Then the *Deuel* sailed toward its final destination — Iwo Jima. Located between Saipan and Japan, this tiny eight-square-mile island of volcanic ash, limestone, and sand was a vital piece of land during the war. The Japanese had built airfields on it, so their fighter planes could intercept Allied bombers. The island's radar stations gave up to two hours' warning of bombing runs over the Japanese mainland. The Allies needed to capture those airfields and radar stations, so Allied planes could carry less fuel and more bombs on their raids over Japan.

The Marines knew the invasion would be incredibly difficult

to pull off. More than 22,000 Japanese were willing to defend the island to the death. They had dug hundreds of tunnels and trenches, reinforced hundreds of natural caves, and built 600 concrete pillboxes designed so they could shoot in any direction. At the southern end rose Mount Suribachi, a dormant volcano upon which the Japanese had placed their big guns to repel any attack from below.

On February 18, 1945, more than 70,000 Marines on dozens of ships prepared for battle. Among those anxious to attack was a young Marine who had turned 17 just five days earlier. As he stood on the deck of the *Deuel* and gazed at the imposing Mount Suribachi, Jack Lucas knew this was his time.

He had a score to settle with Japan. He sought revenge for the dead and wounded at Pearl Harbor. He personally wanted to kill every enemy soldier within sight. *Draw first blood. Show no mercy.*

He was too excited to be scared, too vengeful to be worried. He rechecked his gear. Grenades, rifle, ammo, canteen, backpack. He thought of his mother, who had remarried. On a small piece of cardboard, he wrote, "Please send to Mrs. Radford Jones, Belhaven, N.C. That is my mother." He slipped the note in his wallet, which contained 16 dollars and pictures from home.

At daybreak, the Navy shelled the island with thousands of tons of artillery. Then dozens of Navy fighters and bombers strafed and bombed the island. Hundreds of launch boats dropped off the first wave of Marines — 30,000 of them — clad in green fatigues and brown camouflaged helmets. By 10 A.M., the beaches were teeming with Marines who surprisingly had met little resistance. The Japanese had planned it that way. Suddenly, from underground locations and from atop Suribachi, the Japanese assaulted the invaders with withering artillery and mortar fire.

At 3 P.M., Jack's division was ordered to hit the island at a spot called Red Beach. As Jack crouched in the landing craft, his heart was pounding so rapidly he could hear his blood coursing through his ears. In the distance, he saw clouds of ash and gunpowder billowing over the island, shaken by constant bombardment. Jack gulped when he looked over the side. Bodies of Marines were washing up in the bloody surf. *No wonder they call this Red Beach.*

His landing craft dropped his unit out deeper than he expected. When Jack stepped off the ramp, he tumbled into chin-high water and slogged his way to the beach. All around him, bullets from heavy incoming fire were slamming into the ground. *Is the next bullet for me?*

He wanted to run like the wind, but he couldn't. Every step he took was a struggle because his shoes disappeared in the black volcanic powder. Dodging explosions from artillery and deadly machine-gunfire, Jack hustled as best he could. Wherever he looked, he saw Marines blown up by land mines and mortar fire. There was no rhyme or reason why one soldier reached cover safely while another, only a few feet away, lay dying or dead. It was all so random.

Jack heard the screams from his fallen comrades piercing through the thunder of the relentless shelling. But he couldn't dwell on the carnage, not if he wanted to stay alert — and, more importantly, stay alive. His sole objective was to kill the enemy. The only way to do that was to keep moving. Run, drop, jump up. Run, drop, jump up.

From one foxhole to the next, the Marines ran in a crouching position, inching their way forward. They moved in fire teams of four men each. Jack's team members, all privates first class, were leader Riley Gilbert of Texas, Malvin Hagevik of Wisconsin, and Allan Crowson of Arkansas.

At dusk, Jack and his comrades tried to enlarge a bomb crater to sleep in, but every time they scooped out ash, more slid down the sides. They settled in as best they could for their first night on Iwo Jima. Although he was exhausted, Jack was too pumped up to get much sleep — not that he could with all the flares lighting up the sky and the threat of a nighttime banzai attack from the Japanese.

At daybreak, Jack was feeling confident. He had survived his first day of combat without a scratch. His nerves were on edge, but he wasn't really afraid. *I feel lucky. I'm going to help us take this island.*

His division headed north in an attempt to capture the Japanese airfields. The resistance was much stronger than the day before, but the Marines steadily advanced. Jack spotted a Japanese soldier stepping out from behind a bush and shot him. Jack had always imagined that he would feel an exhilarating rush after his first kill. But he felt nothing like that. He wasn't happy that he had slain the enemy or sad that he had killed another human being. It was just something he had to do to survive. *Kill or be killed.*

When the Marines advanced on the first airfield, the battle grew worse. The Japanese laid down deadly fire from the trenches, scurrying from one pillbox to another through their maze of tunnels. Jack and his fire team leaped into the first of two 22-foot-long trenches that ran parallel to each other several feet apart.

Suddenly, enemy soldiers stood up in the other trench and opened fire on them. The four Marines, keeping their heads down, blindly fired back. Jack kept pulling the trigger as bullets zipped overhead. *Kill or be killed.*

In the midst of the firefight, his M-1 rifle jammed. He kneeled in the trench and tried to fix his weapon. Just then, out of the corner of his eye, he saw two grenades land a few feet away from him. He knew that, at the most, a grenade would explode four seconds after its pin had been pulled.

"Grenade!" he yelled.

His mind raced at breakneck speed. *If the grenades explode, we'll be seriously injured or killed. If we're injured, the Japanese will come in and finish us off. If I throw myself on the grenades, I'll die, but the others will have a chance. Either way, I'm a goner.*

It never occurred to him to run. While still on his knees, he used the butt of his rifle to ram one of the grenades deep into the ash. Then he dived on top of it. At the same time, he grabbed the other grenade with his right hand and pulled it beneath him and then pushed it into the powdery dirt.

The deafening blast hurled Jack up above the trench, turning his body 180 degrees. His eyes wide open, he saw his comrades running for cover. Then, for a brief moment, he felt totally at peace. He heard no noise. He felt no pain.

But then he came crashing down to the ground on his back, and all his senses returned with a vengeance. His ears rang so loudly they muffled the soldiers' shouts and gunfire. His nose twitched with the acrid smell of explosives. His eyes burned from falling dust and dirt. His mouth tasted of blood. And the pain — slowly building from numbness to excruciating agony — marched through all parts of his body.

I'm still alive. How is that possible? Two grenades go off, and I'm still alive?

He turned his head to the right. *My arm! Where's my arm? Was it blown off?* He blinked and squinted. *No, it's still there, thank God.* He discovered that his right arm was pinned underneath his back.

With great effort, he lifted his head and saw that his clothes were in shreds and smoking. His entire body was riddled with bleeding shrapnel wounds from the size of a BB to that of a nickel. Slivers of wood from the stock of his rifle were embedded in his chest. He knew his right lung had been punctured because he could barely breathe. He felt like he was suffocating. *I survived the blast, and now I'm going to die. How long does it take for a body to bleed out? I don't want to die. I'm not ready.*

Gasping and coughing, he uttered in barely a whisper, "God, please save me! Please save me, God!"

The three men whose lives he saved had killed eight Japanese soldiers in the other trench and then moved on, believing Jack was dead. After all, no one could have survived after falling on a live grenade.

And so Jack lay there alone in agony, hanging on to his life, hoping someone would find him, someone other than the Japanese. He couldn't move any part of his body other than his head and the fingers on his left hand. "Help! Help!" He tried to shout, but the words came out in a hoarse, gurgled mumble. No one heard him.

With each passing minute, his chances for survival dimmed. He tried not to panic, but it wasn't easy. With his uniform in tatters and covered with blood, he wondered if anyone would recognize him as a Marine — a live Marine who needed immediate help.

Finally, a fellow soldier from another company approached him. Jack wiggled the fingers on his left hand and mouthed the word *American.*

The soldier kneeled next to Jack and said, "Geez, you're alive." He cupped his hands and yelled, "Medic!"

A corpsman lugging a huge pack of medical supplies rushed over to Jack and gently pulled Jack's right arm from under his body. Although it was mangled, the arm was still firmly attached. Then he gave Jack a shot of morphine to ease the pain and began treating the wounds.

Looking up, Jack saw a Japanese soldier emerge from a nearby cave. With all his might in his weakened condition, Jack choked out, "Jap behind you!"

The corpsman, who was carrying a carbine (a lightweight rifle with a short barrel) along with his medical supplies, wheeled around and shot and killed the enemy soldier, who was about to lob a grenade at them.

"Thanks," murmured Jack. "You've saved my life twice."

Boom! Boom! Boom! The ground shook and dirt flew. "Mortar attack!" yelled the corpsman. He leaned over Jack's body to protect him from flying debris.

Will I ever get out of this place alive? Jack wondered. Shells exploded closer and closer to them, but luckily the bombardment stopped, and two stretcher bearers rushed in and picked him up.

Jack looked down into the trench and saw his ripped backpack, his busted-up rifle — and a Japanese grenade that he had shoved under his body. *It didn't go off! Through the grace of God, the second grenade didn't blow up! No wonder I'm still alive.*

He was taken to the beach where hundreds of the wounded lay in their own personal misery. Given another shot of morphine, Jack lost consciousness. When he awoke hours later, he was on the hospital ship *Samaritan.*

"Son, we've operated on you," said the doctor. "You've got a long road to recovery, but I think you're going to make it. I guess you're just too young and too tough to die."

Because the ship was filled beyond capacity with wounded soldiers, Jack's bed was above deck. About midday on February 23, someone yelled excitedly, "Hey; they've raised the flag on Suribachi!" Ships blasted their horns in celebration and in support of the troops, who still had more difficult fighting ahead of them.

Jack raised his head slightly and looked out over the ship's railing. In the distance he saw the Stars and Stripes waving in the breeze atop Mount Suribachi. *We've taken the high ground! We're going to win!* His head plopped back onto his pillow, and he grinned. He had never been more proud to be an American.

Over the next several months, Jack underwent 21 operations on his right arm, right leg, and chest. His extraordinary bravery and his astonishing actions to save the lives of his three fellow Marines made the news around the world.

On October 5, 1945, on the White House lawn, President Harry S Truman presented the Medal of Honor to Jack — the youngest recipient of that award since the Civil War. Truman told Jack, "I'd rather be a Medal of Honor winner than president of the United States."

Jack joked, "Sir, I'll swap with you."

True to his word to his mother, Jack, who still had about 200 tiny pieces of shrapnel in his body, finished high school and graduated from college. He was married three times and ran a meatpacking business. He wrote a book about his life called Indestructible: The Unforgettable Story of a Marine Hero at the Battle of Iwo Jima, *which supplied some of the material for this story.*

The Americans needed 36 days to capture Iwo Jima, a critical battle that sent the Japanese reeling toward defeat. The toll to secure the island was high: 6,821 Americans dead, 19,000 wounded. Of the 22,000 Japanese who defended the island, 20,000 died.

American Bushido

LIEUTENANT RICHARD ANTRIM

The prisoner-of-war camp reeked from the smell of raw sewage. Ditches, fences, and barbed wire ringed the perimeter. So did stone-faced Japanese guards, some wielding rifles, others carrying bamboo canes to beat prisoners.

Carved out of the jungle near the port city of Makassar on the Indonesian island of Sulawesi, the compound was dotted with hundreds of open-sided bamboo huts lined with wooden boards down each side. These were the captives' stark quarters. In the main area, more than 2,000 prisoners — American, British, Australian, and Dutch pilots, sailors, and soldiers — milled around in their tattered, sweat-stained clothes and bare feet. They looked hungry and weary.

Jumping off one of the prison trucks that rumbled to a stop in front of the camp, U.S. Navy Lieutenant Richard Antrim waited for the rest of his group, 150 captured sailors from the USS *Pope*. "Gentlemen," he said grimly, "welcome to your new home."

"It's not exactly the Ritz," cracked Lieutenant Ben Wilson. No one laughed.

"No talking!" snapped a Japanese officer.

Following orders from his captors, Antrim marched his men into the compound, their heads held high in a show of naval pride. As the gate closed behind them, each man wondered when — or if — he would ever return home.

"Prepare yourselves for the worst," Antrim warned the men. "The only way to survive . . . ouch!"

The officer dropped to one knee after a guard whacked him hard on the back with a long cane and hissed, "No talking!"

Like each new prisoner, Antrim was forced to take off his boots. Then he was herded to a chair where his hair was cut off with a pair of dull clippers. Antrim gritted his teeth when he reluctantly obeyed orders to turn over his wedding ring, the watch his wife, Mary Jean, had given him, and his wallet, which held cherished pictures of his daughters — Judy, nine, and Nancy, seven — back home in Peru, Indiana. Antrim wondered, *Will I ever see them again?*

Antrim had been serving as executive officer on the *Pope* when Pearl Harbor was attacked. In those first few months of the war, the Japanese ruled the South Pacific and Indian Ocean with a massive force of cruisers, destroyers, and aircraft carriers. Facing such an overwhelming armada was the Allies' Asiatic fleet, a much smaller collection of old rusty ships, including the

Pope—a creaky four-stack destroyer, which the crew liked to say "was old enough to vote."

The 32-year-old veteran sailor and Naval Academy graduate had displayed cool leadership during two sea battles in which the *Pope* and three other ships sank three enemy vessels and damaged several others.

On March 1, 1942, the *Pope* was escorting two damaged British destroyers, the *Encounter* and the *Exeter*, off the coast of Java when they were attacked by Japanese planes and eight enemy ships. Antrim and his fellow sailors aboard the three Allied vessels knew they didn't stand a chance. But they were determined to go down fighting.

The *Pope* opened fire on the closest enemy destroyer and then laid down a smoke screen, so the Japanese couldn't see where to shoot. Under Antrim's guidance, the *Pope* scored a direct hit on the destroyer, sending up a column of thick smoke and causing it to turn away. The men cheered until their own vessel came under brutal fire.

The Japanese ships moved in on the three destroyers, which were now zigzagging in a desperate attempt to avoid getting hit. As the enemy bore down, Antrim launched nine torpedoes. One of them struck a cruiser, but he and his crew were too busy to celebrate. They were fighting for their lives.

Twenty minutes later, Antrim's heart sank when he saw both the *Exeter* and the *Encounter* suffer direct hits and begin to sink.

Then six Japanese planes roared overhead and dive-bombed the *Pope*, each taking two turns at trying to blow it out of the water. The plucky Americans fired their machine guns, hoping to drive them off. It was no use. A bomb exploded off the bow (front), knocking out a gun and injuring two gunners. Another bomb near the stern (rear) ripped open a hole below the waterline and severely damaged one of the two propeller shafts, forcing the ship to slow down.

Antrim rushed belowdecks to the stern where water was gushing into the engine room and rear compartments. He quickly organized two teams — one to pump out the water and the other to repair the hole. But despite the frantic actions of the crew, the flooding couldn't be contained.

Returning to the bridge, Antrim told Commander Welford Blinn, "The stern is settling fast. There's no way we can save her."

"Prepare to abandon ship," Blinn said as a dive-bomber made another pass at the crippled, sinking vessel.

Antrim immediately ordered his men to open all watertight doors and ports to hasten the scuttling of the ship before the Japanese could capture it. He then arranged to have confidential records and secret underwater sound gear destroyed by a demolition charge. After ordering the lowering of a large lifeboat, Antrim checked on the final plans to blow up the engine room. Meanwhile, the radio operator was transmitting an SOS.

Everything was ready. As the last enemy plane — spent of bombs and bullets — headed off into the dusk, Blinn ordered, "Abandon ship!"

By now, water was lapping over the deck by the stern. The injured men were put in the lifeboat while most of the crew hopped into three life rafts. A demolition expert then blew up the engine room and scrambled into a raft. Within minutes, shells from two distant Japanese cruisers slammed into the *Pope*.

After the last explosion, the ship's stern slid under the water. With a final gasp, the bow shot up and then plunged straight down until it disappeared below the surface 15 seconds later.

No one said a word. Finally, with a lump in his throat, Antrim whispered, "She was a good ship." *This is no time to get sappy*, he scolded himself. "All right, men, let's lash all the rafts to the lifeboat." He held muster to confirm that all 151 crewmen had survived. (One died before the *Pope* sank.) Because there wasn't enough room in all the rafts or lifeboat, they had to take turns floating in the water in their life vests.

Thanks to the SOS signals, Allied planes had driven off the Japanese cruisers, so the men were hopeful of a rescue before they were captured. As night settled in, Antrim divided the crew into six watches to look out for the enemy, a rescue ship, or a friendly submarine.

A flare was set off at 10 P.M. but there was no response. "We won't be here long," said Antrim. "Help will arrive soon. You'll see."

Later the next afternoon, the men's hopes soared when they heard a plane approach. But their happiness turned to alarm when they saw the insignia on the wings — the Japanese rising sun. The plane circled over the crewmen but didn't fire on them and flew off.

Knowing the pilot would inform the closest Japanese ship of the survivors' location, Antrim thought, *If we don't get picked up soon by our side, the Japs will get us in the next day or two.* He didn't say anything to the men, figuring they had come to the same conclusion. With every minute, he could tell they were getting increasingly restless and tense. *I've got to say something to build morale.*

"We'll get picked up tomorrow for sure," Antrim announced. "In fact, I'll give ten bucks to the first man who spots the rescue ship." He snapped his fingers. "Hey, I've got an idea. Let's have a pool. Everyone bet a dollar, and I'll write down your guess of the exact time we're rescued. The one closest to the actual time gets the dough."

That lifted their spirits. To further increase their chances of rescue, the boat's motor was started up, and the overcrowded rafts and floating men were towed toward Java. Land was still not within sight when they ran out of gas about noon of the third day. Antrim helped rig a sail with a blanket at the bow. Then, aiming the boat in a southerly direction, the strongest officers, including Antrim, and crewmen rowed in relays with all available paddles and oars.

For the second time, the men's hopes were raised and then dashed late in the afternoon when another enemy plane circled them. By nightfall, life jackets of those men in the water had become so waterlogged they were almost useless. Many sailors were nearing exhaustion from treading water or from hanging on to the sides of the rafts.

Antrim spent part of the night swimming from man to man, calling out their names to make sure they hadn't slipped below the surface. Several times, he had to dive under and rescue a fatigued sailor who had let go of the raft. The lifeboat was now dangerously overloaded with worn-out men.

At 10:30 P.M., a sailor shouted, "Ship off the starboard bow!"

In the darkness, Antrim spotted the lights of a vessel heading toward them. At first, he felt relief. *Finally!* But then he wondered, *Friend or foe?*

"Looks like I'm gonna be a hundred and fifty bucks richer," crowed the sailor who first spotted the ship.

Antrim used a flashlight to signal the ship in a special code. If it was a friendly vessel, it would respond in the same code. *I hope she's on our side.* He waited and then signaled again. The suspense made everyone hold his breath. It was so quiet even the light swells seemed to stop lapping against the rafts. *Friend or foe?* Finally, a flashing light from the ship responded to his signal. His heart sank.

"It's the Japs!" he announced.

Before the groans and cussing of the men grew louder, he ordered, "Everyone on the starboard side, grab a paddle or an oar! Hard to port! We have to evade the ship!"

His body shaking from lack of sleep and exhaustion and no small amount of fear, Antrim dug his paddle into the water and pulled. "Stroke . . . stroke . . . stroke . . ." Then he ordered everyone to be quiet while they continued to paddle in rhythm.

Looming closer was a Japanese destroyer, its powerful searchlight beam crossing back and forth across the black water. Closer and closer. And then . . .

"They found us!" a sailor cried out in the glare of the beam.

A Japanese officer hailed them. Lieutenant Ben Wilson, who spoke Japanese, answered, and announced that yes, they were the crew of the USS *Pope*. All 151 Americans were taken aboard as prisoners and transported to the Makassar POW camp on Sulawesi.

At the camp, Antrim and his men lived in open bamboo huts like the other inmates. Everybody was issued one blanket, which they could use as a pillow or a cover. Even though it was hot and stifling, most men wrapped themselves in the blanket at night to protect against the maddening mosquitoes that constantly tormented them. During the day, the huts teemed with strange bugs and spiders that left welts on the men from stings and bites.

Their diet consisted of pap rice — which had the consistency of wallpaper paste — for breakfast and steamed rice for lunch and again for dinner. They became so hungry that certain insects became delicacies to eat. Their only meat came from capturing and killing rodents. No private fires were allowed in the camp, so the men secretly did their cooking in holes dug under the boards of their beds.

Trying to stay healthy — just trying to stay alive — was a constant struggle for the captives, who fell victim to diseases such as dysentery, malaria, hookworm, and ulcers. Antrim suffered from all those illnesses, and his once strapping frame withered to skin and bones.

Each morning, the prisoners had to line up for muster. At sundown, they had to bow to the west in honor of the Japanese sun god. During these forced gatherings, an English-speaking Japanese officer fed them propaganda — lies designed to weaken the prisoners' resolve: "Your wives and girlfriends are cheating on you." "Your families are disgusted by your cowardice." "There is no more baseball in America." "Start learning Japanese, so you will be prepared when we take over the world."

The Japanese further tried to demoralize the prisoners by publishing *The Dia Nippon,* a newspaper printed in English and filled with lies. Every issue featured false stories of how the Japanese had successfully invaded Australia, destroyed the Allies' Asiatic fleet, and occupied Hawaii. "Remember, gentlemen," Antrim told his crew, "read this paper for what it really is — pure fiction."

Somehow Antrim dealt with the hunger, pain, illness, insects, and lies. But it was the constant abuse that tore at his soul. Torture was common, arbitrary, and sometimes deadly. Day after day, Antrim watched sadistic guards beat prisoners for the most minor of infractions, such as not standing straight during roll call or sneezing when a camp official walked by. Antrim did his best to avoid eye contact unless spoken to directly by a guard, because the Japanese were looking for any excuse — not that they needed one — to inflict pain on a prisoner.

Sometimes at night, Antrim heard the cries of tortured prisoners. He lost count of the times he would wake up and find a bloodied body sprawled on the ground — the handiwork of vicious guards with nothing better to do than to beat an American to death.

Every morning he prayed, *Just get me and my men through the day.* And every evening he prayed, *Just get me and my men through the night.* Like the steamy heat that blanketed the camp, fear smothered the prisoners. Would they be the next one tortured? Would they be the next one killed?

Antrim understood why brutality was a daily part of life at the camp and talked to his men about it. "They will abuse us every chance they get," he warned. "They view us as inferior to them because we surrendered. Surrender is not an option to them. They believe in fighting to the last drop of blood. To them, getting captured is worse than death."

Lieutenant Wilson stepped forward and said, "This mentality is called Bushido. It means 'the way of the warrior' — an ancient code that demands endurance, courage, and honor. A warrior who has been taken prisoner has forfeited his honor and should take his own life. To live in captivity is to live in dishonor. That's why they hate us so much and view us as subhumans. They think we are cowards and unworthy of their respect."

One day in April 1942, about six weeks after he was captured, Antrim spotted a group of prisoners standing sullenly in a circle. He heard heart-wrenching yelps of agony and the sickening sound of bamboo striking flesh. He hurried over and saw a guard thrashing a prisoner, an Australian officer.

"What happened?" Antrim whispered to a British sailor.

"The Aussie didn't bow low enough to satisfy the Jap," the sailor replied out of the corner of his mouth.

The raging guard had unleashed a series of violent blows that knocked the officer to the ground, opening up gashes on his head, back, and arms. Other Japanese rushed to the scene and egged on the guard to continue the abuse. They also kept a cold eye on the growing crowd of prisoners who stood by helplessly. The captives had learned that the slightest attempt to help their fallen comrade or the mere utterance of disapproval of the beating would draw attention to them. And then they would face a similar, or possibly worse, fate than what the Australian was suffering.

The guard was in a frenzy, relentlessly beating the officer, who by now was curled up on the ground and barely conscious.

My God, thought Antrim, *when is that Jap going to stop this insanity? He's killing the Aussie. I can't let this go on any longer!* The righteous anger that had been building inside him for this and all the other senseless beatings finally exploded. "Enough!" Antrim shouted. "Enough!" He stepped forward, his hands outstretched as he pleaded, "Have mercy on this man!"

The prisoners gasped that one of their own had broken a cardinal rule in the camp — he had called attention to himself. The guard stopped and glared at Antrim in disbelief. The other guards closed in on Antrim. He tried to ignore them.

"You've punished him enough," Antrim said. "Can't you see you're killing him? The officer meant you no harm. He bowed to you in a show of respect. Yet you've beaten him within an inch of his life. Where is the honor in that?"

Seeing the commotion, the commandant of the camp stormed into the center of the increasingly large circle that had formed around Antrim, the guard, and the battered Australian. The furious guard talked excitedly to the commandant, motioning to the Aussie and to Antrim.

They'll probably kill me for what I've done, Antrim thought.

But I can't back down now. If I have to die, I'd rather it's because I'm trying to save a life.

The commandant spun on his heels and faced Antrim. "My guard says this man dishonored him and deserves the punishment. Yet you have taken it upon yourself to claim we are too severe. We Japanese are a fair-minded people. I will hold a trial right here in front of everyone, and then we will judge whether this man has received the proper punishment."

What the Japanese held was a kangaroo court — a mockery of justice in which the outcome had already been decided. Acting as a judge, the commandant listened to the irate guard describe how the Aussie had insulted him by not bowing properly. The Aussie had regained consciousness but was too injured to speak in his defense. Antrim wasn't allowed to testify because he hadn't witnessed the actual "offense."

"I have heard the evidence," the commandant announced. "The prisoner is guilty of showing a total lack of respect for one of my men. He was being punished when you" — he pointed to Antrim — "interrupted the guard. Taking that into consideration, I have decided on a just sentence for the offender — fifty lashes."

Antrim started to protest, but the commandant cut him off. "Don't say a word, and step back!" he ordered.

The guard picked up a hawser, a thick piece of rope, whirled it over his head, and then whacked the Aussie in the head. The officer crumpled to the ground. Again and again, the guard struck him while the prisoners glumly watched in silence. Soon three more guards joined in the brutality, kicking the prone officer, who was once again beaten into unconsciousness.

I can't stand here and watch him die like this, Antrim thought. *I've got to do something right this second!* Without thinking of his own well-being, Antrim waved his arms and shouted, "Stop! Stop!"

The guards paid him no heed. The prisoners groaned, fearing that Antrim had just signed his own death warrant. The commandant thundered, "Shut up!"

Now what? thought Antrim. In a flash, it came to him. "I'll take the rest of the lashes!"

The guards stopped their beating. Silence fell over the camp. The commandant walked up to Antrim and said, "What did you say?"

Antrim looked him right in the eye and calmly replied, "I'll take the rest of the lashes for him."

"Why would you carry out this act of personal sacrifice for a man who isn't even your nationality?"

"Because he is a fellow human being, a fellow officer. Because he is my brother, like all the other men in this camp."

Hearing the words of their courageous officer, the prisoners erupted in a roaring cheer for Antrim. They didn't care that their actions could lead to severe punishment. They felt a need to show their support for a man who so strongly believed in humanity.

The commandant wheeled around and ordered the guards to take the Aussie to his hut. Confused and stunned, the guards carried out the order in silence. The commandant stared at Antrim long and hard.

What's he thinking? Antrim wondered. *What's he going to do?* Antrim tried to read the commandant's eyes for a clue. *Am I going to get beaten? Am I going to be executed?*

The commandant walked away.

The prisoners crowded around Antrim, patting him on the back, thanking him for taking a stand. He had brought them hope that mercy still could be found in this terrible camp. Antrim's brave action won new respect from the prisoners — and also from the Japanese. The guards began thinking that maybe American military men were honorable and bold after all. Proving himself a leader, Antrim became a spokesman for his fellow POWs and convinced the Japanese to improve camp living conditions. Torture and abuse eased over the next months. Buffalo meat and sweet potatoes became a part of their diet.

But three years later, when the war turned against Japan, conditions worsened and the brutality returned. The prisoners were ordered into forced labor. One of their tasks was constructing trenches for protection during air raids.

When the commandant put Antrim in charge of this detail, Antrim wondered, *How can I turn this to our advantage?* That night, he heard bombing in the distance. *The Allies are getting closer.* And then it dawned on him. *I know exactly what to do!*

The next morning, he went to the commandant and told him of a better way to design the trenches. Antrim's plan was approved. *If they discover what I'm really doing, they'll torture me first and then behead me. But it's worth the risk.* He was convinced his plan would save the lives of countless prisoners who might otherwise be accidentally bombed.

The POWs dug the trenches in a pattern that couldn't be

recognizable from the ground. But from the sky, where the Allied bombers were flying, the ditches were easy to spot and gave a clear signal they had been made by prisoners. Under the eyes of their clueless captors, Antrim and his men had dug trenches that spelled out two giant letters — *US.*

After three and a half years of captivity, Antrim was freed with the rest of the survivors of the POW camp in August 1945 when the war ended. He returned to the Navy, was awarded the Medal of Honor for his selfless actions, and retired in 1954 as a rear admiral. Antrim settled with his family in Mountain Home, Arkansas, where he ran a small tour-boat business. He died in 1969 and was buried in Arlington National Cemetery. In 1981, the Navy commissioned a guided missile frigate and named it the Antrim *in honor of a noble hero who took a stand for humanity.*

Attack in the Devil's Sea

Commander
Lawson "Red" Ramage

Commander Lawson "Red" Ramage peered through the periscope of his submarine, the USS *Parche*, searching for signs of a Japanese convoy in the heavily traveled waters off the coast of Taiwan. It was June 1944 in a battle-active area that the sailors called the Devil's Sea.

"See anything yet, Captain Red?" asked quartermaster R. L. Daufenback.

The commander chuckled and said, "Nothing but a 'sky lookout' perched on the number one periscope. Can't tell what kind of bird he is, but his toilet habits aren't very proper."

Puffing on his pipe, Ramage stepped away, his wavy red hair nearly touching the ceiling. More than a few Navy men questioned why a tall officer such as Ramage would volunteer for duty in a cramped submarine. Salt water seemed to flow through the veins of the 35-year-old officer from Beaver Falls, Massachusetts. A Naval Academy graduate, Ramage made the Navy his career and decided that the best way to become a commander was to volunteer for service as a submariner. Never mind that it was the riskiest branch of the Navy — one out of every five U.S. subs sank during World War II.

At Pearl Harbor, Ramage had taken over command of the *Parche* (pronounced PAR-chee). It was named after a small, brightly colored tropical fish that swims upside down or on its side through intricate coral reefs. (All American subs at the time were named after fish.) The football-field-long sub had a crew of 66 and 10 torpedo tubes — six in the bow and four in the stern.

As a commander, Ramage was easygoing and friendly. But whenever it was time to fight the enemy, he was all business and expected his crew to perform with 110 percent effort. After all, this was war.

Living conditions in subs like the *Parche* were awful. The air smelled of a foul mixture of cigarette smoke, toilet fumes, diesel fuel, and body odor. Fresh water was at a premium, so the men didn't bathe as often as they'd have liked.

Their sleeping quarters was a room packed with tiny triple-layered bunks with so little space between the levels that the sailors couldn't sleep on their sides. The torpedo men slept on bunks that were either suspended over or beside the torpedoes. Because space was at a premium, there weren't enough bunks for everyone, so in some cases three men shared two bunks. While one was on watch, the other two slept. They called this arrangement "hot bunk" because when a man came off watch to sleep, he often got into a bunk that was wet with sweat from the guy who was taking his place.

The crew worked in shifts, four hours on and eight hours off. In their free time, the men wrote letters, listened to music, or played cards or games such as checkers or backgammon on boards they had drawn on the floor. For a break, Ramage read in his own tight quarters, which featured a bunk, small desk, chair, fold-up washbasin, and a safe where he kept secret documents.

Working shoulder to shoulder in such a confined area was stressful, so Ramage tried to make life in the sub as tolerable as possible. Because it was usually hot inside, he let his sailors wear shorts and sandals and go bare chested. He rarely made them put on their uniforms.

The *Parche* was on a two-month war patrol with the USS *Steelhead* and USS *Hammerhead* in a wolf pack — a group of submarines cruising together, looking to sneak up on enemy vessels and torpedo them. Patrol runs played havoc with the crew's mental toughness. Although most days were boring as the sub glided along an empty ocean, the men remained alert, prepared to act on a moment's notice if the enemy was sighted. Whenever that happened, the next minutes and hours would swirl in terror and heart-stopping battle action.

On this latest patrol, the men were somewhat relaxed. Because a bad storm was stirring up the waves, the *Parche* submerged. It was always a challenge for the sub's two cooks and one baker to keep the pots and pans on the stove during rough seas. Nevertheless, they prepared full meals that included ham, turkey, roast beef, or steak. They baked pies, cakes, cookies, and the crew's favorite, caramel rolls — all in an incredibly small four-foot-by-five-foot area.

At dinner the night of the storm, baker Bob Hall brought out a cake that was four inches thick on one side and only one inch thick on the other. "Sorry, Captain, for how this angel food cake looks. But it was in the oven when we made an unexpected dive, and that's why the cake leans to starboard."

"No need to apologize, Hall. This is not an imperfect angel food cake. It's a perfect 'angle' food cake." Ramage then took a bite. "Mmm, mmm. Delicious."

Hall walked away smiling.

The next day, after the *Parche* had surfaced, Ramage stood on the bridge of the conning tower (the structure above the deck), gazing out over the choppy water. Next to him, one of the men was handing the garbage down to cook J. T. McGuire, who was on the deck, dumping the trash over the side. But then McGuire lost his balance when a large wave crashed into the submarine, and he toppled into the water.

"Man overboard!" shouted the other sailor.

Ramage leaped from the bridge and onto the deck just as another wave picked up McGuire and shoved him back toward the sub. Clutching onto the railing with one hand and leaning over the side, Ramage grabbed McGuire by the arm and yanked him onto the deck. Then the captain held him as another wave washed over them. Helping him to his feet, Ramage guided the shaken cook to the ladder that led to the bridge.

"I don't know how to thank you, Captain Red," sputtered McGuire. "You saved my life."

"It's a life worth saving, McGuire. You're the best cook in the fleet."

"But what if I wasn't a good cook?"

Winking, the captain replied, "It's a long swim back to Pearl Harbor."

A week later, the *Parche* sighted a small Japanese patrol boat and gave chase on the surface. Under Ramage's guidance, the gunners fired the sub's deck guns until the riddled patrol boat caught fire and began to sink. Seeing six survivors scramble into a life raft, Ramage ordered the *Parche* to pick them up.

As the sub moved next to the raft, the Japanese made it clear they didn't want to come aboard. "What should we do with them, Captain?" asked Daufenback while crewmates trained their machine guns on the survivors.

"Well, if the Japs don't want to take advantage of our hospitality, let's wave good-bye and go on our way," Ramage replied. So the *Parche* left the Japanese to fend for themselves in the open water.

Shortly after midnight on the Fourth of July, the *Parche* encountered three Japanese vessels — a large destroyer and two heavy cruisers. "I think we should introduce these ships to our torpedoes," Ramage said from the bridge. "Battle stations!"

As the sub closed within range, the destroyer opened fire first with a salvo followed almost immediately by several shots from the cruisers. Three artillery shells exploded on the port side of the *Parche* and one off starboard, all within 100 yards.

"That's a little too close for comfort," said Ramage. "All hands below! Dive! Dive! Dive!"

Two blasts from the diving alarm sent the lookouts, quartermaster, and officers scurrying off the bridge and leaping down the hatch into the conning tower and into the control room. In less than 30 seconds, the bridge was cleared, and the watertight hatch was secured.

The *Parche* initiated a crash dive, and as the conning tower went under the surface, another round of shells exploded only 20 yards away, shaking the sub.

"Take her down to two hundred feet!" Ramage ordered.

Like all submarines, the Parche used ballast tanks to change its buoyancy (floating ability). Adding water to its tanks caused the sub to go under. Blowing water out of its tanks raised it to the surface.

After the vents were opened to allow water into the ballast tanks, the bow angled down and the *Parche* headed toward the safety of the ocean floor. But the Japanese had no intention of letting the sub get away, and all three ships steamed to the area where the *Parche* had submerged.

"Brace yourselves for depth charges," Ramage told the crew. Moments later, a watertight barrel filled with highly explosive material set to detonate at a desired depth was dropped from one of the ships. *Ka-boom!*

"Go to two fifty," Ramage said, referring to the depth.

Ka-boom! Ka-boom! More depth charges exploded near the *Parche*. "They're right over us. Take her down to three hundred."

The ships above, each with sound-detection equipment, were trying to get a fix on the sub's exact location and depth. The Parche had reached its maximum depth. "Prepare for silent running," said Ramage. The crew shut off the air-conditioning, fans, and all other nonessential motors, so the sub could float quietly near the bottom without being detected. It was crucial that the crew remained silent and moved softly and slowly like cats. *Ka-boom!*

Maintaining stillness played on the men's nerves, including Ramage's. Without fans or air-conditioning, the temperatures soared to more than 120 degrees. Even worse, the crew could hear the enemy's propellers above them. To Ramage, the sound of each ship was like a train crossing a railroad trestle. It started out as a hum, then increased rapidly in volume as it drew closer, before fading after passing overhead.

The ships took turns dropping one depth charge after another at the sub. The men could hear the splash as each deadly charge hit the water, followed by the click of the detonator. They would then brace themselves for the explosion that came seconds later. *Ka-boom!*

The blasts were coming faster . . . and they were getting closer. With each explosion, Ramage's ears rang and his head pounded. It was like being inside a giant bell while someone struck it with a huge sledgehammer. *Ka-boom! Ka-boom!* The shock from the blasts burst lightbulbs, loosened pipes, cracked the glasses on gauges, and shattered a mirror. The lights kept flickering, and the sub kept groaning.

"How much more pounding can the *Parche* take without splitting her hull?" asked one of the sailors. "Should we try to make a run for it?"

Ramage shook his head. "If we do, the Japs will know where we are, and they're faster than us. We have to sit tight. Our best defense is depth and silence." He looked at the terror in the eyes of his men in the control room. Some of them were praying, with their hands clasped; others were fingering crucifixes and Stars of David that dangled from chains around their necks. "We'll get through this. Stay calm."

That was easier said than done. How could you remain cool when you're trapped 300 feet underwater in a cigar-shaped steel tube that the enemy is trying to blow up? *Ka-boom! Ka-boom!* During dangerous times like this, Ramage couldn't help but think about his wife, Barbara, daughters, Joan and Virginia, and son, James. *God, I miss them. But I'll get home one of these days. I just know I will.*

Ka-boom!

Soon the sound of the propellers of the Japanese ships began to fade. They had left the area. An inspection by the relieved crew revealed minor damage to the *Parche*, which surfaced at nightfall.

"I lost count of the number of depth charges after seventy," said Daufenback. "Happy Fourth of July, Captain Red."

In his logbook, Ramage wrote, "Our Fourth of July was officially recognized, with the Japs providing the fireworks."

There were more fireworks to come — only the next time, Ramage would ignite them. On the night of July 31, shortly after the *Hammerhead* had left the wolf pack, the *Steelhead* attacked a convoy in the Devil's Sea and scored several hits. Then it withdrew to reload its torpedo tubes. Now it was the *Parche*'s turn.

At 3:20 A.M., Ramage stood on the bridge and counted 13 Japanese ships, including three antisubmarine escorts, six miles away. Twenty minutes later, the convoy shot two white flares into the sky to light up the area in an attempt to detect any enemy vessels.

"Damn," said Ramage. "Looks like we've been found by one of the escorts. It's heading our way."

"Should we take her down, Captain?" asked Daufenback.

"I refuse to be driven below. I've got a better idea. We're going to work our way into the convoy."

"On the surface?"

"Yes."

"So it will be the *Parche* against more than a dozen Jap ships?" Seeing a fiery, determined look in the commander's eyes, Daufenback said, "Sounds good to me."

Actually, it sounded like a foolhardy plan, but Ramage believed that by boldly slipping into the midst of the convoy, he could create enough havoc and confusion to sink several ships. He just hoped one of the stricken vessels wouldn't be his own.

"Everyone to battle stations!" he ordered.

Never had he felt more alive, more aware, more confident. Or more angry. *The Japs are going to pay a heavy price for starting this war,* he told himself. "I'm going to sink all of you!" And then he launched his daring night action.

Under Ramage's direction, the *Parche* eluded one escort, sneaked past two others, and took a bead on an armed transport ship. He needed to attack the vessel before the escort next to her had a chance to shoot at the sub. He fired two torpedoes at her, but the transport managed to turn fast enough to avoid getting hit.

"We missed!" Ramage peered through his binoculars and

soon his frown changed into a smile. When the transport turned sharply, she moved right into the path of her escort, effectively blocking the escort from firing at the sub. The maneuver also opened up a great opportunity for Ramage to attack not only the transport but also two nearby tankers.

He fired a torpedo and watched with gleaming satisfaction as it slammed into the hull of the transport. A plume of water spewed up and then the ship exploded. He had scored a direct hit. "Gotcha!" he crowed.

Turning his attention to the closest tanker, he launched four torpedoes. "Go get her, fish!" he said, talking to the torpedoes. He felt the usual slight jerk of the sub as the high-pressure air expelled the torpedoes from the bow tubes. He followed their wakes. *Looking good. Looking real good.* Then he saw four geysers, one after another, along the side of the ship. *Boom! Boom! Boom! Boom!* The entire tanker exploded in a huge fireball that lit up the sea.

"Oh, what an absolutely beautiful sight!" he shouted, beaming in the glow of the fire. "Now let's do the same to that other tanker. Right full rudder!" he ordered. The *Parche* swung hard until the stern tubes were lined up on the second tanker. "Fire one! Fire two! Fire three!"

The first torpedo skirted past the tanker's bow, but the other two struck the ship's forward section. Unfortunately, she didn't blow up. But Ramage could tell that the tanker had been damaged and was slowing down.

He reserved any further gloating for later because now he faced a new danger. Two escorts, firing deck guns, machine guns, and flares, were bearing down on the *Parche*. "Clear the bridge!" he ordered. "Daufenback, you stay here with me. The rest get out. I don't want anyone else getting shot at and ending up on eternal patrol [dead]." The two lookouts and the two officers who had been standing next to him hurried down the hatch.

Everywhere Ramage looked he was surrounded by Japanese ships, many of them zigging and zagging, trying to escape the crazy American commander while others were roaring toward him. Exposed by the light of bursting flares and bravely defiant of shellfire passing close overhead, Ramage felt invincible. Everything he tried was working. Now he was ready for his boldest — and most dangerous — move of all.

"Let's reload right now," said Ramage.

"During battle?" said Daufenback. "But it's never been done before."

"Well, there's a first time for everything. We have a crackerjack crew, and I have great faith they can do it."

Noting that the commander was still flashing that confident look, Daufenback said, "I have no doubts you're right, Captain Red."

Normally, after launching 10 torpedoes, the sub would dive out of harm's way and reload in calm waters. But Ramage wanted to fire more torpedoes at the targets around him right now. The reload crews, though, had to worry about wrestling bulky 600-pound torpedoes into firing tubes while the sub was maneuvering this way and that way at full speed. One misstep, and a torpedo could detonate, sending the *Parche* and everyone in it to a watery grave. The torpedo men in the stern had it the worst. They could barely stand because the sub was turning left and right so wildly. They rubbed the small statue of Buddha that they kept in their compartment for good luck.

Back on the bridge, Ramage saw a medium-size Japanese merchant ship steam into view, guns blazing. "Looks like she wants to ram us. Bad move." Ramage fired two torpedoes. "Bull's-eye!" he shouted moments later. It took less than five minutes before the vessel disappeared below the waves.

With that ship out of the way, Ramage was determined to finish off the crippled tanker. When the *Parche* drew within 500 yards, the tanker fired on the sub, but her heavy guns couldn't aim low enough to cause any harm. However, small-arms fire peppered the bridge, forcing Ramage and Daufenback to take cover. At 800 yards, Ramage fired three more torpedoes. All hit the tanker with terrific explosions that ripped open the hull. She listed to her side and went under, leaving behind only a small oil fire.

Ramage was now focused on the biggest prize of all — a huge transport. But first he had to contend with two escorts off the port bow that were concentrating their machine-gunfire at the *Parche*. The sub turned away from them, but right into the path of another escort off the starboard side.

"She's trying to ram us! Full bell! Full bell!" he shouted, ordering the engine room to go full speed. The sub shot across the bow of the onrushing Japanese vessel. "Right full rudder!" The stern of the *Parche* swung around so that the sub was now beside and parallel to the escort, but heading in the opposite direction.

The two vessels passed within a breathtakingly close 50 feet of each other. The Japanese sailors leaned over the side and, thrusting their arms in the air, began yelling and cursing at Ramage. The captain tipped his cap and sarcastically yelled back, "Enjoy the rest of the evening, you slime buckets, because it'll be your last!"

The *Parche* wasn't out of danger yet. Ramage found his sub boxed in on both sides by the other two escorts that were firing at him. Adding to his dilemma, the big transport was dead ahead and steaming right for the sub.

"Everybody wants to ram us tonight." He took a deep breath. "I've got to fire straight down her throat." There was no other way. It required a perfect shot at the narrowest part of the ship. Anything less and the *Parche* would be crushed by the huge transport. "Fire one!" To his dismay, the first torpedo drifted off to the right. Time was running out. Ramage made a quick adjustment and yelled, "Fire two! Fire three!"

He held his breath. *Come on, fish, come on.* Both torpedoes sped head-on and slammed into the bow of the transport, stopping her cold.

"Way to go, Captain!" Daufenback shouted. "Shall we get out of here?"

"Not yet. I want to finish her off." Closing in on the transport's starboard bow, the *Parche* swung hard left and fired one stern shot at 800 yards for another bull's-eye. "Damn it, why won't she go down?" He maneuvered the sub, preparing for another shot when suddenly the transport raised her stern into the air and went straight down, headfirst into the cold depths of the ocean.

"I think we've had enough fun tonight," said Ramage. "Time to leave this party."

As the sub weaved away from the stricken convoy, bewildered Japanese were still firing weapons in the darkness at the submarine — and mistakenly at each other.

The *Parche*'s amazing attack lasted 46 hair-raising minutes. Ramage had fired 19 torpedoes and scored 16 hits. He damaged or sank five vessels.

Later that morning, Ramage addressed his men. Many of them had been so busy performing their duties during the attack they had no idea what had happened. The men cheered when they learned of the damage they had caused the convoy.

"I have never been more proud of a crew," Ramage said. "I am honored to be your shipmate."

They roared their approval. But the loudest ovation came when he told them that because the *Parche* was out of torpedoes, the sub would be returning to Pearl Harbor. For the crew, that meant two weeks of fun and sun on the beaches of Hawaii.

For his utter fearlessness, daring, and extraordinary tactical skill in attacking a Japanese convoy at night and on the surface, Ramage was awarded the Medal of Honor in 1945. He was later promoted to vice admiral and became one of the Navy's most decorated submariners. In 1990, Ramage died at his home in Bethesda, Maryland, and was buried in Arlington National Cemetery. Five years later, the Navy commissioned a new guided missile destroyer and named it the USS Ramage in his honor.

Hero Without a Gun

Private First Class
Desmond Doss

Desmond Doss knelt by the side of his barracks bunk and began to pray silently, knowing what would happen next. Halfway through his prayers, fellow soldiers erupted in hoots and catcalls directed at him:

"You better be praying to get out of the Army 'cause we don't want you!"

"Hey, you coward. Why don't you ask God for some backbone."

Doss kept praying.

Acting like a chicken, another soldier folded his arms and flapped them as he waddled over to Doss and chirped, *"Bwawk, bwawk, bwawk."* Then an army boot flew past Doss's head.

Doss kept praying just as he did every night during basic training. He ignored the taunts of his own platoon that had been harassing him ever since he enlisted. The soldiers disliked him because he was different. The slightly built private strictly followed his religion as a Seventh-Day Adventist — a belief often at odds with the military. It meant he refused to touch a weapon or do anything on Saturday other than pray, because in his faith that was the Sabbath, a day devoted to God.

Growing up in Lynchburg, Virginia, Doss attended Bible classes with his younger brother and older sister because his father, a carpenter, and his mother, a shoemaker, were devout Seventh-Day Adventists. On the wall in the living room of their home was an illustrated poster of the Ten Commandments. The picture beside the sixth commandment, "Thou Shalt Not Kill," showed Cain killing his brother, Abel — the first murder recorded in the Bible. Doss became so moved by the picture that he vowed he would never take the life of a human being or an animal, no matter what. He wouldn't even eat meat, because it would have meant slaughtering one of God's creatures.

When World War II broke out, Doss, then 22, was working at a shipyard in Newport News, Virginia. Because he was in an industry considered essential to the military, the Army had no plans to draft him. However, Doss wanted to serve his country in the military, but in a nonviolent way. He was willing to go into combat only if he could tend to the wounded as an unarmed medic. Accompanied by his minister, he enlisted as a conscientious objector — a person who refuses to bear arms because of religious beliefs.

Before Doss left for basic training in 1942, he married his fiancée, Dorothy Schutte. On their wedding day, she gave him a pocket-size Bible, so he could read scripture every day. It was his most treasured possession.

At Fort Jackson, South Carolina, new recruits were taught how to kill with a variety of weapons. But Doss refused direct orders to shoot a weapon in target practice, although he went through all the other training. On Saturdays, while the others sweated during rigorous workouts or disgusting duties like cleaning the latrines, Doss read his little Bible because it was the Sabbath. He tried to make up for those Saturdays by working and training extra hours during the regular week.

Nevertheless, his fellow soldiers quickly grew to resent him and displayed their hostility by ridiculing and cursing him every night when he knelt beside his bunk and prayed. The bullying hurt him, but if nothing else, he showed them that he was a strong-willed man of faith.

Doss's convictions didn't impress his commanding officer, Captain Jack Glover, who became fed up with him. "Private, I've had it with you," fumed Glover. "You're a soldier, yet you won't train on Saturday or shoot a gun or carry a bayonet. And you won't eat meat."

"Sir, I entered the service as a medic. I enlisted to heal, not to kill."

"Even medics must be trained to shoot the enemy," Glover countered. "We're in the middle of a war, Doss. Soldiers must be willing to kill or else they jeopardize combat missions and the lives of their comrades. We need to rely on one another and cover one another's back. If you're not willing to protect your own men, then you don't belong in the military. You're a misfit,

Doss. I've started the paperwork to declare you unsuitable for military service on the basis that you are unstable and have mental problems. Dismissed!"

At a hearing to determine if Doss should be kicked out of the Army, the earnest private gave a passionate defense in front of the top brass. "I want to serve my country, even though I refuse to kill," he said. "I've performed all of my other duties with dedication and I've been an exemplary soldier in every other way. I love my country — a country that prides itself on religious freedom. Isn't that one of the reasons we are at war — to protect our freedoms? Yet you want to give me a dishonorable discharge by claiming I'm mentally unstable for no reason other than I am practicing my religion. I'm sorry, gentlemen, but that is flat out wrong and un-American. And you know it."

The officers on the hearing board admitted that Doss was right. He returned to his unit, the Seventy-seventh Infantry Division, and completed his training as a medic. The men in his platoon weren't happy and continued to taunt and tease him. One day, a big, beefy soldier nicknamed Goon blocked Doss's path to the barracks. Pointing to Doss's head, Goon hissed, "When we get into combat, the first bullet I fire will be aimed right there."

Fortunately, the soldier never carried out his threat. When the unit was shipped to the South Pacific in 1944 to fight the Japanese, Doss showed how courageous and forgiving he really was. During heavy fighting at Leyte in the Philippines, the unarmed Doss braved enemy gunfire to reach the wounded and get them out of harm's way so he could treat them. Time and again, he showed his compassion for the very men who had despised him by rescuing them under a hail of bullets. For his repeated heroism, Doss earned the Bronze Star — and the growing respect of his comrades. No one mocked him anymore for reading his little pocket-size Bible during lulls in combat.

In April 1945, the Seventy-seventh Infantry Division landed on Okinawa, an island held by the Japanese. In order to capture the island, the Americans needed to take control of the Maeda Escarpment, a 400-foot-high cliff that stretched across Okinawa. On the top, which flattened out for several miles, thousands of well-armed, entrenched Japanese waited to fight the Americans from caves, tunnels, and camouflaged machine-gun nests.

Preparing for a tough battle, the men of the Seventy-seventh hiked up the steep, rugged escarpment for the first 360 feet. The final 40 feet required climbing up Navy cargo nets that had been strung across the sheer cliff face.

When the order was given to rush up and over the top and attack the Japanese, Doss told Lieutenant John Goronto of Company B, "I believe prayer is the best lifesaver there is. The men should really pray before going up." Just a year earlier, such a suggestion would have triggered a chorus of jeers. But now, the men had completely changed their thinking from condemnation to admiration for their faith-based medic.

"Fellows, come over here and gather around," Goronto ordered. "Doss wants to pray for us."

That's not what Doss had in mind. He was only suggesting that each soldier take a moment for personal, private prayer.

The men turned toward Doss and bowed their heads. He closed his eyes, cleared his throat, and said, "Dear Lord, please help the lieutenant give the right orders, because our lives are in his hands. Give us the strength and courage to succeed in the name of freedom. Grant us the wisdom to be careful and to look after one another. Amen." He opened his eyes and told the men, "I hope each of you makes his peace with God before going up the cargo net. May God bless every one of you."

While the men from Company B climbed the cliff, their comrades from Company A were doing the same thing a half mile away. When those troops stormed over the top, they were met by intense gunfire from the Japanese. Five men from Company A were killed within seconds, and the rest of the unit was pinned down, unable to advance. As the casualties mounted, Company A was forced to retreat and scurry back down.

But Company B doggedly fought on, advancing slowly but steadily while facing ferocious resistance. From behind a large rock, Doss waited to charge out in the open at the first cry of "Medic!" He watched with amazement as his unit swept across the area, knocking out nine pillboxes and routing the Japanese from their hiding holes. By the end of the day, the Americans claimed victory in the first of many brutal battles on the escarpment. What was so remarkable was that not a single member of Company B was killed or even wounded, except for one soldier whose hand was injured by a falling rock.

When headquarters learned of Company B's stunning, casualty-free success, they asked Lieutenant Goronto the reason why they won. The officer pointed to the unit's skinny medic and said, "Because Doss prayed."

Although the Americans had won the first round, the Japanese refused to retreat fully from their rocky fortress. Over the next few days, they pounced out of their caves and tunnels in vicious counterattacks. Doss risked his life time and again to save his fellow soldiers on the bloodstained escarpment. Despite being exposed to heavy rifle and mortar fire, he crawled 200 yards forward of the lines to rescue a wounded soldier. Two days later, he watched four men get cut down while they were assaulting a strongly defended cave. Doss advanced through a shower of grenades to within eight yards of the enemy's cave and dressed his comrades' wounds before making four separate trips under fire to evacuate each of them to safety. Later that day, another American was severely wounded 25 feet from an enemy cave. Ignoring the gunfire, Doss crawled to him, rendered aid, and then carried him 100 yards to safety.

The fiercest fighting erupted on May 5. Enemy artillery, mortars, and machine-gunfire raked the men of Company B as Japanese soldiers swarmed out of their foxholes and caves from every direction. Within minutes, dozens of Americans — about half the company — fell wounded. The Japanese attack was so strong that the remaining men from Company B were forced to retreat to the base of the cliff. The only soldiers remaining at the top of the escarpment were the wounded, the Japanese, and Doss.

He peered down over the edge of the cliff where the rest of the unit had gathered. Then he looked over at the dozens of troops who were bleeding and sprawled on the ground. *They're my men, and I can't go off and leave them — even if it costs me my life,* he told himself.

As shells burst around him and bullets whistled past his ear, he low-crawled out toward the closest wounded soldier, bandaged the man's leg, and half carried him to the edge of the cliff. Doss then took a thick rope and fashioned a sling, which he put around the soldier. Next, Doss wrapped the rope around a tree stump once and then carefully lowered him 40 feet to the waiting arms of the troops below. *That's one down* — he scanned the area and sighed — *and way too many more to count.*

He scurried over to the next downed man and dragged him to the edge and lowered him to safety. Dodging bullets and grenades, Doss raced from one fallen comrade to another, helping or lugging or carrying each one away from the line of fire and then easing him down by feeding the rope hand over hand. Hour after hour, he kept pulling the wounded from the field of battle. Others who were hit managed to work their way back to the edge of the cliff and fought off the enemy while waiting their turn to be lowered by Doss.

His hands raw from gripping the rope and his arm muscles shaking from exertion, Doss wasn't sure how much longer he could continue. As he lowered each soldier, Doss silently prayed, *Lord, help me get one more. Just one more.* And then he would zigzag his way through a burst of gunfire to rescue another and another and another. With each rescue, he found himself closer to the enemy, but Doss couldn't stop trying to save lives. *Just one more.* Many of the wounded who were still fighting provided cover for the gutsy medic. He couldn't worry about bullets and grenades, because if he did, he knew he would be too scared to attempt another rescue. So he stayed focused on getting the next soldier off the summit. *Just one more.*

Although weary and almost to the point of exhaustion, Doss persevered. *I couldn't live with myself if I left anyone behind.* And so the one-man rescuer continued to push himself beyond what he thought was possible. He hauled the remaining half-dozen fallen soldiers to the edge of the cliff and started lowering them one at a time.

By now, some advancing Japanese had crept within a few yards of Doss and were poised to kill him. But two of the wounded Americans spotted them in the nick of time and shot them. Doss quickly lowered the last of the injured and, after securing the rope, slid down and collapsed on the ground below from sheer exhaustion.

Doss had been rescuing his men nonstop for five straight death-defying hours. When he was finished, the medic who the Army didn't want had single-handedly saved the lives of an estimated 75 soldiers. Accepting pats on the back and shaking hands with grateful comrades, Doss wobbled off to a quiet spot behind a large boulder and slumped to the ground. *Thank you, Lord.* Then from his shirt pocket, he pulled out his little Bible and began to read.

The battle for the Maeda Escarpment was far from over. On the night of May 21, the Americans launched a bold attack, and Doss was once again ready to help tend to the wounded. The Japanese laid down withering fire, forcing the Americans to take cover.

But when Captain Glover, the company commander, was felled by machine-gunfire, Doss dashed out into the open and unhesitatingly braved enemy shelling and small arms fire to assist the officer. Doss applied bandages, moved his patient to a spot that offered protection, and while artillery and mortar shells fell close by, painstakingly administered plasma. When litter bearers finally arrived to take Glover away, the captain clutched Doss's hand. Although it was hard for him to talk because of his injuries, Glover uttered, "Thank you for saving my life. The man I tried to have kicked out of the Army ends up being the most courageous person I've ever known. How's that for irony?"

"You were only doing what you thought was right," said Doss. "And I'm doing what I know is right."

Doss then joined three other soldiers in a shell hole while he waited in the night for the next shout for help. Moments later, he heard a soft thud in the hole. "Grenade!" shouted one of the troops. Three men scrambled out of the hole, but Doss reacted too slowly. The grenade exploded near his right leg, hurling his body out of the crater. When he fell back to the ground, he passed out. Regaining consciousness, he said a quick prayer and then checked his leg. It was still there but bleeding badly.

Weak and going into shock, Doss gave himself an injection and bandaged his own wounds, using the medical supplies that he carried. Tracer bullets and grenades continued to riddle the area. *No sense calling for another medic*, he thought. *Why should I make him leave his cover and risk his own life for mine? I'll just stay here until this fight is over.*

He lay in pain for five long hours before two litter bearers found him at dawn. They began carting him away on a stretcher when he spotted a soldier slouched against a tree, suffering from an open chest wound. "Stop! Stop!" Doss shouted to the bearers. "Put the litter down right here." When they did, he rolled off the stretcher and grimaced in pain.

"What? Are you crazy?" one of them said.

Pointing to the critically wounded soldier a few yards away, Doss said, "He's in much worse shape than I am. Take him first and then come back for me."

While Doss awaited their return, a big, burly soldier whose head and thigh were bleeding came over to him and knelt. "Put your arm around me," said the soldier. "I'll help you get to the medical station." Slinging his rifle over his shoulder, the soldier helped Doss up. "Now just lean on me."

"Thanks." Doss put his arm around the soldier's neck and then cracked a huge grin. He had just realized that the man he was leaning on was Goon, the guy who had once threatened to kill him.

"Why are you smiling?" Goon asked.

"You know, God really does work in mysterious ways."

Bang! Bang! Bang! Rifle fire from a sniper broke the morning calm. Doss screamed out as a sharp pain ripped through the arm that he had curled around Goon's neck. Doss let go and crumpled to the ground. Goon quickly dragged him behind a rock.

"A sniper got me in the arm," Doss winced. The bullet had struck him in the wrist, deflected through his elbow, and then lodged in his upper arm.

"I'll be right back," said Goon, who then crawled off to a nearby bush. Seconds later ... *Bang! Bang!* Goon scurried back. "You won't have to worry about that sniper anymore."

"Mind if I borrow that rifle?"

"You of all people want to shoot my rifle?"

"No, I'm not going to shoot it. I'm going to use it as a splint." Gritting his teeth from the pain, he had Goon help him use the rifle stock to fashion a splint for his seriously wounded arm.

Once again, Goon helped Doss up, and they hobbled back toward the aid station 300 yards away. On the way, Goon stopped, faced Doss with a look of wonder, and said, "You know what's really weird?"

"What?"

"If you hadn't had your arm around my neck when the sniper shot at us, that bullet would have nailed me right in the neck. I'd probably be dead."

Doss smiled through his pain. "Like I said. God works in mysterious ways."

After they reached the aid station, Doss was put on a stretcher. As he waited to be taken to a hospital ship offshore, he reached into his shirt pocket for his Bible. "Oh, no!" he groaned. "It's lost!"

He called over a soldier. "Please, please, pass the word around that I lost my Bible. It's really important to me. My wife gave it to me on my wedding day, and it's been my constant comfort through all the combat. Will you ask the guys to look for it when they finally drive the Japs off the escarpment? I know it's a long shot, but could you ask them? Please?"

"Sure, I will." The soldier didn't have the heart to tell him that Doss's Bible would be virtually impossible to find on the battlefield — especially one where fighting was still going on.

On the hospital ship, doctors removed 17 pieces of shrapnel from Doss's leg and put a cast on his shattered arm. He eventually returned to the United States, where he spent several months in the hospital recovering from his wounds.

Hailed as a hero, Doss was summoned to the White House, where on October 12, 1945, President Harry Truman presented him with the Medal of Honor. Desmond Thomas Doss became the first conscientious objector in American history to earn such an honor.

Doss told reporters, "I loved my men, and they loved me. I don't consider myself a hero. I just couldn't give up on them. I feel that I received the Medal of Honor because I kept the Golden Rule: Always treat others as you would like them to treat you."

When Doss returned to his home, a package from the Seventy-seventh Infantry had arrived. Inside were a small box and a note that read: "After we defeated the Japanese on the Maeda Escarpment, the entire battalion fanned out and conducted a search of the battlefield until we found what we were looking for. We know you would want this." He opened up the box and began to cry. The men who had once mocked him for his religious beliefs had mailed home his lost Bible.

Doss, who moved to Rising Fawn, Georgia, suffered poor health because of the lingering effects of his war wounds, and was in and out of hospitals for six years. Tuberculosis in both lungs, contracted during his service in the Pacific, left him unable to work full-time. Despite his health problems, Doss volunteered at local organizations, helped with Seventh-Day Adventist scouting programs, and talked to groups about the war. He died in 2006 at the age of 87.

Flying Blind

SERGEANT FORREST "WOODY" VOSLER

Army Air Corps Sergeant Forrest "Woody" Vosler had just arrived at a base in Molesworth, England, and was nervously awaiting his first mission as radioman on a B-17 bomber of the 358th Bomb Squadron, 303rd Bomb Group, Eighth Air Force.

Known as Flying Fortresses and each manned by a crew of 10, the four-engine B-17s flew risky missions. They had to fly through rough weather to Germany, evade swarms of machine-gun-firing fighter planes of the *Luftwaffe* (the German Air Force), and then dodge deadly flak (bursting artillery shells) that filled the skies. Those bombers lucky enough to reach their target and drop their three-ton payload then faced more flak, more enemy fighters, and often more bad storms on their return to England's fog-shrouded airfields.

Crews who completed 25 missions earned a trip back to the United States. But Vosler knew the average life expectancy of an Eighth Air Force B-17 in late 1943 was only 11 missions. *Will I ever make it home alive?* the 20-year-old airman wondered.

During his first three days at Molesworth, Vosler watched hundreds of B-17s take off on bombing runs inside Germany. Every time, about 30 planes failed to return, and another 30 were so crippled they barely made it back to the base.

When it's my turn to fly, will I be up to the task?

Vosler got his answer a week later on his first mission. He was assigned to the crew of a B-17 called the *Jersey Bounce Jr.*, led by Lieutenant John Henderson, the pilot, and Merle Hungerford, the copilot. Navigator Warren Wiggins and bombardier Woodrow Monkres shared space in the nose of the plane and were responsible for plotting the route and accurately dropping the bomb load. They also had to defend the craft with two .50-caliber machine guns. On the top of the Flying Fortress and directly behind the cockpit was Bill Simpkins in a rotating Plexiglas bubble. His job was to drive off enemy fighters by firing twin machine guns. Farther back in the fuselage (the plane's main body) was Vosler. When not manning the radio, he was expected to shoot his own machine gun from a nearby roof hatch. Behind the radio room and beneath the fuselage was the clear Plexiglas sphere of ball-turret gunner Ed Ruppel. In Ruppel's cramped and dangerous position, he defended the plane's belly. Above him on the left and right side of the fuselage were waist gunners Stan Moody and Ralph Burkart, each responsible for firing a machine gun out the side hatches. In a tiny crawl space in the tail was George Buske with his twin machine guns.

On November 26, 1943, the *Jersey Bounce Jr.* joined more than 500 heavy bombers on a mission to destroy enemy installations at Bremen, Germany, in one of the largest single-day American air assaults yet mounted. Protecting the lumbering bombers were more than 300 fighter planes.

As the *Jersey Bounce Jr.* climbed to 27,500 feet, the crew put on their oxygen masks. At that high altitude, the temperature had plunged to 50 degrees below zero. Despite heavy leather jackets and pants, both lined in wool, Vosler was shivering. But it was more than just from cold. He was terrified. *Just do your job,* he told himself.

Ice began building up on the windows, making it hard to see. Adding to the danger, thick white contrails (streams of ice crystals that look like smoke) flowed behind each bomber, offering possible cover for enemy fighters sneaking up from behind.

When the Flying Fortresses neared Germany, the tension mounted. More than 50 enemy fighter planes attacked in packs, trying to pick off one bomber at a time.

"Looks like we've been greeted by the welcoming committee," Henderson coolly cracked to his crew over their interphones. "Let's show 'em what we think of 'em."

Machine-gunfire from the *Jersey Bounce Jr.* echoed throughout the cabin, even through Vosler's earphones. *Focus on your work,* he told himself, unable to stop his trembling. *Let the others do their job and hope for the best.*

Fighting off his fears, he busily attended to his radio. But then he noticed that the waist guns had fallen silent. He left his radio and found Moody and Burkart sprawled on the floor. *They've been hit!* He turned them over but didn't see any blood or wounds. They were turning blue. It was then he realized that their oxygen system had been knocked out, causing them to lose consciousness. As enemy aircraft took aim at the men who were exposed at the open side hatches, Vosler grabbed portable oxygen bottles and revived his comrades. They went back to their posts and fended off the fighters while their plane completed the bombing run.

The *Jersey Bounce Jr.* returned to the base safely. But although the bombers and escorts in the group shot down 70 enemy fighters, 25 bombers and four escorts were lost.

Vosler had come through just fine in his first taste of combat. In fact, the officers of his squadron were so impressed, they awarded him the Air Medal for his quick-thinking actions that saved the two waist gunners.

But he still fought fear with every flight, especially during the crew's fourth mission on December 20. The target was once again Bremen, which was encircled by a half-mile-wide ring of antiaircraft guns and was protected by additional fighter planes. He knew it would be the most dangerous mission yet for his crew.

Shortly after the *Jersey Bounce Jr.* joined up with hundreds of other planes for the massive bombing run, the first wave of more than 100 enemy fighters attacked them over Holland. For a frantic hour, the German planes zoomed in from the left and right, firing their machine guns. They soared above the formations and dropped small explosives on the bombers below.

In groups of three or four, the Germans attacked the B-17s from the side while American escorts valiantly fought them off. Meanwhile, heavy flak pockmarked the sky.

From his radio hatch, Vosler fired at the screaming fighter planes. To his horror, he watched two stricken bombers explode. Then another B-17 caught fire and dived sharply before crash-landing in a field. Seconds later, flak knocked out the engines of another B-17, forcing the crew to bail out. Vosler knew that if those airmen survived, they would be caught by the Germans and shipped to a prisoner-of-war camp.

The *Jersey Bounce Jr.* miraculously evaded the flak and the onslaught of fighters to reach the target where Monkres shouted "Bombs away!"

"I love hearing those words," Vosler declared. His hopes of a safe mission soared as Henderson turned the B-17 to the north, away from the battle and out toward the North Sea. But then in the midst of a flurry of flak, the sturdy bomber shuddered and began to lose power. "Uh-oh," muttered Vosler.

From the ball turret on the plane's belly, Ed Ruppel shouted into the interphone, "Number one is on fire! I see holes in the left wing, and flames are shooting out!" The plane banked hard to the left and went into a steep dive. The rushing air soon put out the flames on the far left engine, leaving a slight trail of smoke behind the wing.

Just when Vosler and the others started relaxing a bit, flak took out the number three engine on the right side and destroyed much of the instrument panel in the cockpit. With two engines out, the plane slipped away from the protection of the large formation.

Other bombers that had been struck had also fallen behind and became easy targets for the German fighter planes. Vosler saw four crippled B-17s under attack, including one that was a hundred yards away when it blew apart from enemy fire. The Germans chopped up another bomber and another. They sent the fourth one into a tight death spiral.

Now that the fighters had knocked the four disabled bombers from the sky, Vosler knew that the *Jersey Bounce Jr.* was next. When the plane descended to 15,000 feet, Vosler looked out and thought, *Oh, no. The entire Luftwaffe is after us.*

Bullets peppered the lone B-17, creating a loud pelting sound as if the bomber were flying through a hailstorm. From the tail, Vosler heard George Buske cry out in pain over the interphone, "I'm hit!" A 20-mm shell from a diving enemy fighter had exploded in the bomber's tail section, hurtling deadly shrapnel and pieces of the stricken plane forward through the fuselage.

Before he could dive for cover, Vosler was struck hard below the waist. He stood still for a few seconds, waiting for the terrible pain to surge through his body. When it did, he felt scared, especially when he saw blood flowing down his legs through his tattered pants. *Uh-oh, this looks serious,* he thought. *I've got to do something to protect myself, or I'm not going to make it.* He knew his survival depended on staying calm and acting quickly. He staggered to the radio desk and plopped in his armor-plated chair, which curled up around his back. He hoped it would protect him from further shrapnel while he figured out his next move.

How silly is this? I don't know where the next bullets will come from. If the chair isn't facing the right direction, it won't stop any of them. I might as well stand up and fire my machine gun. Better to die fighting than to die sitting in a chair.

From the open radio hatch, Vosler looked out and felt sick to his stomach. Enemy fighters were roaring toward his plane from all directions. He didn't know which fighter to shoot at first, so he began firing away in a steady stream, praying that some of the bullets would strike the eight German planes now diving toward the lone B-17.

Whatever pain Vosler felt in his bloody legs was dulled by his intense focus on survival.

Fortunately, the bomber's firepower blunted the first attack. As the German fighter planes regrouped, Bill Simpkins left his post on the top turret and scurried to the tail section to check on Buske. As Simpkins made his way to the back of the plane, a German fighter bore in on the bomber. Ralph Burkart unleashed his machine gun, sending the enemy spinning toward the ground, black smoke trailing all the way down. Five minutes later, Burkart blasted another fighter out of the sky.

Meanwhile, in the shattered tail, Simpkins found Buske slumped over his guns, unconscious and bleeding badly. The veteran tail gunner, who had recently returned to combat duty after a 45-day recovery from a severe bullet wound during a previous mission, had been hit in the stomach. His torn flight suit revealed a gaping wound in his chest, which exposed his right lung, diaphragm, and abdomen. After dragging Buske toward the center of the plane, Simpkins tried to give him an injection of morphine to ease the pain. The syringe was frozen from the frigid air, so Simpkins thawed it by putting it in his mouth. Then he gave Buske a double shot of morphine. With Burkart's help, Simpkins applied compress bandages to slow the flow of blood from the jagged opening in Buske's chest and abdomen.

"I can't do any more for George," Simpkins said. "I don't think he's going to make it."

Henderson kept the battered bomber airborne as his gunners, including Vosler, fought off the nightmarish attack. Firing from the left-waist-gun position, Simpkins let loose with a loud "Yahoo!" after his bullets sheared off the right wing of a fighter.

Though the *Jersey Bounce Jr.* was in deep trouble, the crew still believed they could escape the fate of the other downed bombers. Realizing that the most vulnerable part of their plane was the unmanned tail section, Simpkins crawled to the rear. Although the guns were too damaged to fire, he remained there to warn the pilot over the interphone of any attack from behind so evasive action could be taken.

Out of nowhere, a German fighter swooped down on the *Jersey Bounce Jr.*, and Vosler was in the best position to shoot at it. *This is my chance. If I miss, we're probably going down.* The radioman pressed the trigger, and the first burst knocked pieces off the fighter's left wing. Vosler kept firing until the fighter burst into flames and tumbled toward earth. "I got him! I got him!"

He pulled his goggles over his eyes and scanned the sky for more targets. But the goggles fogged up, so he pushed them back up on his forehead. Just then, an incoming 20-mm shell slammed into the breach of his machine gun and exploded.

Vosler fell backward, pain burning in his chest as blood began streaming from a dozen openings in his shredded flight suit.

His eyes stung and his vision was blurred. *They're not playing the game right, hitting a guy in the eyes. Damn, I can't see well at all. How badly am I hurt?* He tried to open his jacket, but when he moved his fingers down to his chest, his hand was shaking. *I can't control my hand. What's happening to me?* Then he reached up and dragged his fingers across his face. When he looked down, he could barely make out that his whole hand was covered with blood.

I've lost the whole side of my face! I only have half a face! He started wailing because he was awash in pain and panic. *I'm not going to get out of this mess now. My life is coming to an end, and there's nothing I can do about it.* The fear of dying magnified the pain, the frigid air, and the unrelenting bursts of gunfire. He crumbled to the floor, curled up in a ball, and kept screaming because only by hearing his screams could he be sure that he was still alive. The crushing terror he felt as death drew near left him gasping for air. *Keep screaming . . . keep scream . . . keep . . .*

He felt numb, and darkness descended over him. Then images of his life appeared in his mind like a mental slide show: learning how to swim in Lake Ontario with his brother and two sisters; becoming a Boy Scout; growing to six feet three inches and playing basketball for Central High in Livonia, New York; working as a drill-press operator after graduation; and enlisting in the Army Air Corps after World War II broke out.

And bribing a sergeant:

"You've passed all the requirements to become a radioman on a bomber except one — you're too tall," says the sergeant. "You can't be over six feet." "I've got a five-dollar bill for you if you put down seventy-two inches on my form," says Vosler. The sergeant pockets the money and replies, "You're on your way to flight status."

And nearly being denied a chance to fly:

Vosler bumps his head on a doorway at a training air base. A captain says, "Hold on, Sergeant. I've seen hundreds of men go through this door, and they don't bump their head if they're under six feet." The captain measures him. "You're way over the height limit, which we have because it's too hard for tall people to get in the turrets of the B-17 and man the machine guns. Each crewman must be able to handle all the gun positions on the plane." "I can do it, sir," Vosler declares. The captain laughs and says, "You really want to fly in bombers, don't you?" "I certainly do, sir." "I'll give you a crack at it. If you can operate the guns from all the positions, more power to you. I'll let you fly on a bomber as a radioman."

Going in and out of consciousness, the dying Vosler had relived virtually every memorable day of his 20 years of life. It put everything in perspective. For the first time, he discovered something about himself: *I've had a wonderful life with a great family. Oh, sure, I've had a few bad days, but mostly it's been pretty darn good. God, forgive me for those bad days, and thank you for all the many good days you've given me. I'm not going to ask you for any more days. You've been very nice to me.* Vosler lifted his hand and blurted, "Take me, God, I'm ready."

A warm feeling of calmness and contentment swept over him. He no longer felt like screaming. He no longer feared death. But then the pain wracked him with an agonizing suddenness. *God, if you're not going to take me right now, then I guess I better get up and do the best that I can.* He tottered to his feet and then slouched in the chair.

Ed Ruppel came over to him and groaned at the sight of the blood-soaked radioman.

"How bad is it, Ed?" Vosler asked. "Give it to me straight. I can't see."

Ruppel replied, "Woody, you've got shrapnel wounds from your forehead to your knees. They're everywhere. Blood is all over you, coming out from all those little shrapnel cuts."

"My face. Do I still have a face?"

"You're a bloody mess, but your face is intact. You might lose your right eye, though. It's really damaged."

"I'm going blind and I'm bleeding all over. Not a good combination."

"Don't give up, Woody."

"I've made my peace with God and I'm ready to die," Vosler told him. "But I have a feeling that God doesn't want me yet, so I'll do what I can to help."

Ruppel looked around the radio room. "Aw, hell, Woody. The radio is all bashed up from the shrapnel."

"Let me work on it. Just patch me up the best you can."

Ruppel wrapped Vosler's wounds and then returned to the turret to continue fighting the waves of attacking fighter planes. The *Jersey Bounce Jr.*, shredded from nose to tail, was losing altitude and flying so low that German soldiers on the ground were shooting at it. The only good news was that the enemy pilots had turned their planes around, apparently thinking the shot-up B-17 would soon crash.

"There's no way we'll make it back to England," Henderson, the pilot, told the crew. "We need to stay airborne long enough to reach the North Sea, so we can ditch this baby."

If they could make it far enough to crash-land in the water, their survival would depend on radio communication with potential rescuers. Although virtually blind, Vosler began repairing his radio just by touch. He remembered what his radio-school instructor had once told him: "A day will come in combat when the job of getting home is up to the radio operator." *He was right,* thought Vosler. *Now it's up to me.*

The pilot ordered all unnecessary equipment tossed out to lighten the load, which would increase their chances of staying airborne long enough to reach the sea. The crew threw out everything not critical to their survival, including guns, tools, and ammunition.

As Bill Simpkins scoured the *Jersey Bounce Jr.* for unnecessary weight, he went into the radio room to check on Vosler, who was tinkering with the radio.

"We're close to ditching," Simpkins told him. "I'm still looking for stuff to throw out."

"Why don't you throw me overboard?" Vosler told him. "I mean it."

"What? Are you insane, Woody?"

"No, I'm quite sane. It makes perfect sense. By getting rid of me, the plane will be one hundred seventy-five pounds lighter, giving the rest of you a better chance of reaching the sea. I can't see. I'm so badly wounded, I'll probably die anyway. I'm no use to you now."

"But the radio. We need you . . ."

"I've got it fixed. Bill, please, throw me out."

"Forget it, Woody. We took off together and we'll land together."

"But the extra weight . . ."

"Okay, here's what I'm going to do." Simpkins took off the radioman's shoes and tossed them out the hatch. "There, you've contributed to the cause."

"What happens if we crash-land on the ground? How am I going to walk?"

"Barefoot."

Simpkins looked out of the hatch. "Hey, Woody, we're nearing the coastline! I see some flak, but it's far enough away from us not to be a threat. Hey — I see whitecaps! We've reached the North Sea!"

"What about Buske?" Vosler asked. "Is he dead?"

"He's unconscious and barely alive, although I don't know how with his injuries. Man, that guy is tough. We have him wrapped up in life preservers, and he's lying on the floor near us."

As the B-17 continued to lose altitude over the North Sea, Vosler tried to send out an SOS. At first, there was no transmission, but he quickly discovered the problem — a loose connection on the transmitter key. He couldn't see clearly enough to make the repairs, so he instructed Simpkins on how to fix it. Most of the crewmen had gathered in the radio room as Vosler tried again to transmit an SOS. They all cheered when he received a response from England. Vosler kept sending out signals until England was able to determine where the *Jersey Bounce Jr.* would ditch. On instructions relayed by Vosler, Henderson set a course that would put the plane down near a Norwegian trawler.

Vosler and the others knew ditching was a dangerous procedure. Of 180 pilots and crewmen of the 303rd who had ditched, only 69 had survived.

"Everyone, press your seat cushions against your bellies," Henderson ordered. "We're going in! We're at four hundred feet . . . three hundred . . . two hundred . . . one hundred. Brace yourselves, boys!"

Henderson eased the plane to wave-top level, watching the rise and fall of the swells to time the moment of impact. Landing in a trough could be fatal, swamping the bomber before everyone could scramble to safety. In the radio room, Vosler remained at his station, maintaining communication with England.

Henderson pulled on the yoke, forcing the plane's nose up so that the tail would smack the water first. The bomber caught the crest of a wave and rode it like a surfer, then shuddered to an abrupt stop that threw everyone in the radio room violently forward. A jumble of shattered glass and steel flew around the crewmen's heads.

Vosler yelped when his injured, bloody body slammed into a bulkhead. He didn't think he could hurt any more than he already did, but the pain kept increasing. Salt water bubbled up from the smashed bottom turret. Time was running out. They had only a few minutes before the plane sank.

As the *Jersey Bounce Jr.* filled with water, the crew hustled out through the hatches, half the men onto the right wing, the other half onto the left wing. Simpkins lifted Buske through the hatch, lay him gently on the right wing, and then helped inflate the three life rafts.

Vosler exited through the right hatch on his own. Although hardly able to make out shapes, he could tell that Buske was sprawled on the wing. But then he noticed that Buske was starting to slip off the wet wing. *He'll fall into the water and could drown*, thought Vosler. Knowing his comrades were busy with the life rafts, Vosler grabbed the antenna wire that ran from the top of the tail to the radio-room window. With his other hand, he clutched Buske around the waist. *Dear God, please give me the strength to hold on and please don't let the antenna wire break.*

Weak from loss of blood and in horrible pain, Vosler strained against the antenna wire while holding the wounded airman. *I . . . can't . . . hold out . . . any longer.* "Help!" he yelled and then collapsed a second before Simpkins and Monkres leaped onto the wing and secured both men.

"It's okay, Woody," comforted Simpkins as he guided him into one of the rafts. "We're safe now. The worst is over."

When everyone was loaded in the life rafts, they pushed away from the sinking bomber. Minutes later, the nose of the valiant *Jersey Bounce Jr.* dipped below the surface, lifting the tail in the air before the plane slipped under the waves. The fishing boat soon arrived to pluck the men off their rafts and take them to England.

Despite incredible odds, Buske survived his severe wounds

and needed nearly a year of surgeries before he recovered and returned to active duty.

Vosler, who was hospitalized for two months because of his injuries, remained blind for nearly eight months. The doctors operated on his eyes and managed to save the left one, but the other had to be removed. Vosler still couldn't see. He then learned that he would receive the Medal of Honor, but the ceremony was delayed until after surgeons successfully restored sight in his left eye.

On August 31, 1944, Vosler stood on the White House lawn where President Franklin Delano Roosevelt presented him with the Medal of Honor. "Son," said the president, "I'm sorry you had to wait for this honor, but I wanted to personally present you with this medal and I didn't want to do it when you were blind. You are a remarkable hero."

After his discharge from the Army, Forrest "Woody" Vosler went to college and then spent 30 years as a counselor with the Veterans Administration (now known as the Department of Veterans Affairs). He retired to Titusville, Florida, where he passed away in 1992. He is buried at Arlington National Cemetery.

Mission Impossible

LIEUTENANT COLONEL JAMES RUDDER

Lieutenant Colonel James Rudder, commander of the Second Ranger Battalion, stared at his top officers and said, "I won't lie. This mission is going to be real tough. But if there is any unit that can pull it off, it's us Rangers." He took a deep breath.

"All we have to do is cross rough water to a tiny beach while under fire from concealed guns. Then we have thirty minutes to climb a one-hundred-foot cliff while the Germans are shooting at us from above. Next, we must knock out six big guns, set up roadblocks, and destroy German communication lines. Then after we do all that, we have to hold the position against any counterattacks from the landward side."

He didn't have to remind the men what would happen if they didn't pull off this seemingly impossible mission. They knew failure could endanger the greatest invasion the modern world would ever know. And failure could spell their own doom.

"This is what we've trained for," Rudder said. "This is why we're the ones chosen to lead Operation Overlord."

It was just after midnight, June 6, 1944, the opening minutes of D-day. Rudder was talking to his officers aboard the HMS *New Amsterdam*, which was transporting 225 Rangers. The vessel was part of the largest armada ever assembled, as more than 5,000 ships carrying three million American, British, and Canadian forces started across the English Channel. Their objective: to invade five beaches along the French coast of Normandy — code-named Omaha, Utah, Sword, Gold, and Juno — in a bold attempt to break Nazi Germany's iron grip on Europe.

But first, six giant 155-mm guns had to be disabled. These guns, which had a range of more than 10 miles, sat atop Pointe du Hoc, a steep oceanside cliff that gave the Germans an unrestricted field of fire onto Omaha and Utah beaches. The dangerous job of disabling the guns was given to Rudder and his men.

The Rangers were considered the best of the best in the military — brave, brawny volunteers willing to try the impossible. They had trained hard for two years under extreme conditions, scaling 150-foot-tall cliffs on ropes while carrying a full battle pack, weapons, and extra ammunition weighing a total of about 200 pounds. Rudder, a rugged no-nonsense 34-year-old former Texas rancher, drove his men unmercifully, believing it was the only way to succeed.

General Omar Bradley, commander of the First Army Group, had told Rudder, "It is the most dangerous mission of D-day. No soldier in my command has ever been wished a more difficult task."

"My Rangers can do the job, General," Rudder confidently declared.

Shortly before dawn, after a pancake breakfast, Rudder and the other Rangers got ready to climb into 11 landing-craft-assault vessels (LCAs) in heavy seas. From another ship miles away, Major General Clarence Huebner radioed Rudder and asked, "Where are you going to position yourself?"

"I'm leading the attack, General."

"You'll risk getting knocked off in the first minutes, and then where's the leadership?"

"Sorry, sir," Rudder replied. "If you order me not to go, I'll have to disobey you. If I don't go, the attack may foul up, and I'll never forgive myself."

After a long pause, Huebner said, "Good luck."

With Rudder's landing craft leading the way, the Rangers headed for Pointe du Hoc 12 miles away in rough water. Waves battered the vessels and drenched the storm-tossed men, who were bailing out water with their helmets while throwing up from seasickness and raw nerves.

Rudder heard a frantic radio call for help — the LCA carrying extra ammunition and food was sinking, and men were drowning. The cries of soldiers struggling to stay afloat tore at Rudder's heart, but he couldn't turn around. *I must keep my focus on our mission,* he told himself. *The entire invasion depends on it.*

Artillery from Allied battleships behind them screamed overhead and slammed into the cliff in bright orange explosions. From the lead LCA, Rudder wiped the saltwater spray from his eyes, stared at his map, and then at the beach. Turning to the British operator of the LCA, Rudder bellowed, "You're going toward the wrong point! Turn to the west. Now!"

This mistake is going to cost us precious time, he thought. *I don't think we can make it up.* The Rangers were supposed to reach the top of Pointe du Hoc by 7 A.M. If they didn't signal from the summit by that time, Ranger reinforcements would be sent to another beach. *We'll be totally on our own, and that means more of my men will die.*

As dawn grew lighter, Rudder could see the dark, massive point jutting out over a narrow strip of beach. The enemy had placed along the beach large twisted pieces of steel and concrete obstacles to hinder the invaders. Suddenly, German guns opened up on the Rangers' boats. Spouts of water blew up all around them and machine-gun bullets pelted the crafts. A second LCA sunk.

When the other LCAs hit the beach at about 7 A.M., the ramps dropped, and men jumped out into waist-deep water, struggling under their heavy equipment. Some Rangers were hit in the water by mortar bursts. Others slipped under the surface when they stepped into craters made by Allied bombs that had fallen short of their mark. Those who slogged to the beach started running toward the base of the cliff. A German machine gun on the Rangers' left flank swept bullets back and forth across the beach, killing or wounding 15 men.

Hearing incoming mortar rounds, Rudder dove for cover in a crater. The blast knocked him off his feet. When he stood up, he saw that his left arm was bleeding from a piece of shrapnel. Gritting his teeth, he pulled out a metal shard and wrapped a handkerchief around the wound. *I can't let it bother me,* he thought. Running from group to group, he shouted, "Move! Move! We're late! Get up the cliff!"

Behind him was Lieutenant Colonel Thomas Trevor, a six-foot four-inch British commando who had helped train the Rangers. As bullets whizzed past him, Trevor calmly walked among the men, encouraging them.

"How can you do that when the Germans are shooting at you?" Rudder shouted to him.

"I take two short steps and three long ones, and they always miss me," Trevor answered. Just then a bullet slammed into his helmet, knocking him down.

Rudder raced over to Trevor and helped him to his feet. The bullet had lodged in Trevor's helmet and only slightly wounded him. Blood trickling down his face, Trevor shouted at the German, "You dirty Kraut!"

The Rangers used special mortars to shoot dozens of ropes with grappling hooks up onto the top of the cliff. Some of the ropes didn't reach the summit because they were too waterlogged, so many Rangers cut handholds in the cliff face with their knives and started free-climbing the sheer ten-story-tall cliff.

The Germans on top fired down and dropped grenades on the Rangers. The enemy also waited until the Rangers were halfway up before cutting the ropes. Men fell 40 or 50 feet, but those who didn't break any bones shook off the pain and started climbing back up again. Many who neared the top were shot from point-blank range.

Next to Rudder, a climber took a bullet in his chest, stiffened, and held on to the rope for a brief moment with one hand. He gave a strange grin and yelled, "So long, Colonel!" and let go, plunging to his death.

The long-range Allied artillery ceased as Ranger after Ranger shouted, "Up and over!" Once they reached the top, the first soldiers engaged in mortal hand-to-hand combat with the Germans, pitching them over the side. Soon the defenders panicked and retreated inland behind several machine-gun nests.

Incredibly, the Rangers had fought their way across the beach and up the cliff in less than 30 minutes. Rudder's Rangers had breached Hitler's European Fortress. But so far they had lost 40 men. When Rudder made it to the summit, he thought, *We all should have been slaughtered, yet so many of us made it. I don't know how we did it. But we did it!*

A quick survey of the landscape left him stunned. He gazed at a bewildering wasteland pitted with so many holes from bombs that it reminded him of the craters on the moon. Underneath a thick layer of smoke, the ground was littered with smashed equipment and the bodies of German soldiers. For months, Rudder and his men had studied the area, using detailed photographs and maps that showed every slight feature of the land. But the bombardment had wiped out expected landmarks, such as paths and buildings. *Great,* he thought. *Now, my men are in danger of losing their way because our maps are useless.*

Nevertheless, he sent out his platoons from Companies D, E, and F to find and destroy the big guns and to establish a roadblock on the major highway that went from the Pointe toward the town of Grandcamp. He also set up a command post in a crater between the cliff and a destroyed antiaircraft gun emplacement.

Hopping from crater to crater, the Rangers moved through minefields and under barbed-wire fences. Within minutes, Rudder heard from one of the platoon leaders. "Colonel, we went to where the guns were supposed to be, but they're not here. The Krauts put telephone poles in their place to trick us. Where could the guns have gone?"

"The Germans probably moved them to a more secure position inland," said Rudder. "Look for tracks and other markings."

Reports were coming in from other platoons that they were under sniper and machine-gunfire. At any given moment, the Germans would pop out of underground passageways, shoot at the Americans, then scurry off in the tunnels to another vantage point and fire away again. While the platoons advanced inland as far as three miles from Pointe du Hoc, they met stronger resistance and heavier artillery fire from the Germans.

Back at the command post, snipers and enemy artillery were harassing Rudder and his men, so he called for one of the ships to shell the Germans. Minutes later, he heard, "Incoming!"

The right side of their command-post bunker exploded. The shock wave lifted Rudder and then slammed him hard to the ground. His ears ringing and head aching from the blast, Rudder staggered to his feet as debris, dirt, and a yellowish smoke swirled around the bunker. He stumbled toward the two men nearest him. One was seriously injured; the other was dead. The dazed colonel slumped down, trying to gather himself.

"Rudder's been hit!" a soldier shouted. "Rudder's hit again!"

As he regained his senses, Rudder realized that his right arm was burning from pain. Blood oozed out of his bicep.

"How bad is it?" a Ranger asked him.

Rudder shrugged. "Just a flesh wound. I'll be all right." He was caked from head to toe in yellow dust from the smoke from a shell that had fallen a few hundred yards short of its target. On the radio, he learned that the shell — a special one that gives off yellow smoke as a marker — had come from the battleship *Texas*.

"Kind of ironic that I, a man from Texas, would get injured by a battleship named after my own state," he told the medic who wrapped the wound in a bandage. Just then, sniper fire forced Rudder and the medic to duck.

Minutes later, Rudder received important news from Company D, Second Platoon: "We've found the guns! We did what you suggested, Colonel, and followed the markings in the ground. They led us into this little valley about two hundred yards from the highway behind a hedgerow. There are five guns here all under camouflage netting and sitting in proper firing condition. The ammo is piled up neatly and fuses are set on the shells and everything is at the ready. All the guns are pointed toward Utah Beach."

"What about the Germans?" asked Rudder.

"It's weird, Colonel. No one is guarding the guns. We've spotted about one hundred Krauts eighty yards away in a corner of the field. They can't fire the big guns because Company E took out their observation post at the Pointe, and we cut their lines of communication."

"Sneak in there and take those guns out with thermite grenades." Rudder was referring to grenades that ignite silently. When the air hits the chemicals of the grenades, white-hot soldering material spews out and fuses everything in its path.

Within 10 minutes, two men from Company D had used the grenades to weld moving parts such as gears, cranks, and hinges so the guns couldn't be aimed. The weapons that posed the greatest danger to the invasion were now useless. (The sixth gun was later discovered in another area, apparently damaged from an earlier bombardment.)

Word soon reached Rudder that his men had blown up the big guns' ammunition as well. It was by now only 8:30 A.M. The pride that Rudder was feeling had all but numbed the pain from his two battle wounds.

He ordered his communications chief, Lieutenant James Eikner, "Send out the message *Praise the Lord*." It was code for "All men are up the cliff and have destroyed the guns."

"Lieutenant," said Rudder, "send another message: *We need ammunition and reinforcements. Many casualties.*"

An hour later, Rudder received a message from General Huebner aboard the *Satterlee*: "No reinforcements available. Other Rangers have landed at Omaha."

Rudder understood why. Because of the rough seas and the navigational error, his Rangers hadn't reached the summit of Pointe du Hoc until after 7:15 A.M. When the reinforcements offshore hadn't heard from the Rangers by 7 A.M., they moved to Omaha Beach four miles away. No one knew how long it would take them to work their way overland to assist their fellow Rangers at the Pointe.

That means we have to hold the Pointe alone, Rudder thought. *The Germans will counterattack. They'll try to drive the rest of us off this cliff.* His men had performed brilliantly so far. But he wondered, *How long can we hold out without more troops and ammo?* He refused to share his worries with his men. Instead, he maintained the cool, calm manner that he had shown throughout this dangerous military operation.

With most of their mission accomplished, Rudder sent word to the platoons to hold their positions until they were relieved, which he hoped would be later in the day. He thought it was important for his platoons to maintain the blockade on the Grandcamp highway, denying that vital road to the enemy.

Late in the morning, the command post again came under sniper fire. "Now I'm really angry," Rudder growled. "Let's kill that Kraut once and for all." He and two of his men slipped out of the bunker and hunted for the sniper, not realizing the crafty gunman was stalking them. The German squeezed off several shots — including one that hit Rudder in the thigh. The commander tumbled to the ground, grimacing, "No, not again!" While one of his men shot at the sniper, the other Ranger helped Rudder hobble back to the command center where he was treated for his third battle wound of the day.

"Maybe you should stay in the command post, Colonel," said the medic who treated him. "Don't you have enough wounds for today?"

"You know what they say," Rudder replied. "Three's the charm."

He sent out another threesome. This time, they killed the sniper.

Reports came in to Rudder that casualties were mounting as the enemy's defense stiffened. Scattered small-arms fire erupted from every direction, and bursts of automatic fire came from a German antiaircraft position only 300 yards west on the edge of the cliff. The situation on the Pointe was still chaotic as Rangers and Germans fought sporadically from crater to crater, often capturing and recapturing each other.

By now, Rudder's men were split into two major groups — about 20 defending the command post and about 60 trying to block the highway. Between the two Ranger groups, hundreds of Germans were getting organized for a counterattack. The rest of the Rangers hadn't made contact with the command post. They were either dead, wounded, captured, or engaging the enemy on their own.

Early in the afternoon, the Germans charged the command post but were repelled. They launched another offensive later in the day, which the Rangers fended off.

An uneasy silence crept over the Pointe as night fell. Trying to stay calm, Rudder took a sip of coffee and asked Colonel Trevor, the British officer, "What do you think will happen next?"

Trevor took a long, deep puff from his pipe and replied, "Never have I been so convinced of anything in my life as this: I will either be a prisoner of war or a casualty by morning."

Rudder nodded and took a bite from a bitter piece of chocolate from his C-rations. "It doesn't look good, does it?

We're holed up on the edge of a cliff with nowhere to go. The Germans are amassing south of the highway, ready to cut off our men there. They have many more weapons, ammo, and troops than we do, so no doubt they'll attack us sometime tonight. Who knows if or when we'll get any reinforcements. Ammo is running low, there is little drinking water, and the only food we have left are these awful chocolate 'dog biscuits.'"

"You see, Rudder, we don't have anything in our favor."

"Oh, but we do, Trevor."

"What's that?"

"We are Rangers."

About 3 A.M., the Germans attacked the command post again. For the third time, the outmanned Rangers held their own. Through it all, Rudder shot at the enemy, coolly directed his men, and ignored the sharp pains from his wounded limbs. When the Germans were driven off, he praised the Rangers. "You are the best in the world!"

Hours later, his faith in his men was shaken when a Ranger from the highway roadblock rushed into the command post and shouted, "The Germans have broken through. We couldn't hold them, Colonel. Guys are getting killed everywhere! About twenty Rangers from Company E were captured. Fifteen soldiers from Company D are hiding somewhere in a field surrounded by a hundred Germans. The rest are in full retreat!"

An hour later, about 50 men from Companies E and F returned to the Pointe, joining the 25 who had been holding down the command center. The number of Rangers on the Pointe had dwindled from 225 to less than 100. How many were dead or captured, Rudder didn't know. But it pained him to think so many would not make it off the cliff alive. Refusing to share his heartache, he talked with each of his exhausted and hungry men, offering them hope that the worst was behind them. Seeing their thrice-wounded commander limping from one end of the command post to the other inspired them.

They needed that enthusiasm because the next day the Rangers were attacked twice more. The gritty Americans successfully held their ground. Because they were getting dangerously low on ammunition, Rudder sent some men out to rummage for the dead soldiers' weapons and ammo. One of the men brought back a big German machine gun that they set up at the front of the command post.

With so little food and water left, Rudder had to ration them. Morale soared late in the afternoon when a Navy boat reached the beach and took away wounded men and prisoners and dropped off some needed supplies. That evening, the Rangers ate jam sandwiches, which to the hungry men tasted as good as a steak dinner.

Shortly after dawn on June 8, the Americans on the Pointe were awakened by German artillery fire. Each hour grew tenser as the enemy moved in closer. Surprisingly, the Germans then backed off. What Rudder didn't know, because all the radios had been knocked out, was that reinforcements from the Fifth Battalion had finally fought their way from Omaha Beach to the highway on the Pointe.

About noon, the Fifth Battalion soldiers, wary that the enemy could still be between them and the besieged Rangers, approached the perimeter of the command post with extreme caution. Believing the troops in the field were Germans, the

Rangers at the Pointe began firing the captured German machine gun.

Not knowing their fellow Rangers were shooting the weapon, the reinforcements assumed the Germans had overrun the command post. So the Fifth Battalion soldiers began firing at the command post with mortars and tank fire.

Rudder's men had endured two challenging days of German assaults, and now they were in danger of being killed by friendly fire. Sensing that something wasn't right — the weapons sounded like American guns — Rudder took a gamble and ordered his men to stop firing. "We're Americans!" he shouted. "Who are you?"

"We're Rangers from the Fifth Battalion!" One head popped up. Then another and another. When the men realized they were all Rangers, they stood up and cheered. The Germans at the Pointe du Hoc had been defeated.

Of the 225 members of Rudder's Rangers who had landed at the Pointe, only 90 were still able to fight when they finally marched wearily but triumphantly from the cliff toward the highway.

Leading his exhausted young heroes, the colonel had mixed emotions. He was incredibly proud that his men had become the first American troops to accomplish their mission on D-day. But as he hobbled across the pockmarked battlefield, where the smell of death lingered in the air, he felt incredible sadness at seeing all the dead Rangers. He had trained them for two grueling years. He knew them by their first names. He knew their strengths and weaknesses. He knew their hopes and fears. And now many of them were dead.

During a break, he told his surviving troops, "I can't begin to tell you how proud I am of you. You helped punch a hole through the formidable Nazi Atlantic Wall. You destroyed the big guns, cut the German communication lines, and held off five counterattacks. I know every one of you would have fought to the last man if I had asked. You accomplished the impossible mission. You are the best. You are Rangers."

Rudder became one of the most decorated soldiers of the war, with honors that included the Distinguished Service Cross. He was promoted to Major General of the U.S. Army Reserves in 1957. Two years later, he became president of Texas A & M University. Rudder died in 1970.

The invasion of Normandy led to the liberation of Paris less than three months later and ultimately ended World War II in Europe. It came at a heavy price for American, British, and Canadian soldiers: 45,000 dead and 173,000 wounded or missing.

General Dwight D. Eisenhower, Supreme Commander of all Allied forces in the Normandy assault, once said, "I had always attached great importance to the liquidation [elimination] of the Pointe du Hoc gun battery. It took guts to get up those cliffs that day."

Today, the battle-scarred Pointe du Hoc remains exactly as the Rangers left it on June 8, 1944, but with one addition. A large stone monument stands in tribute to the men who fought and died there.

The Ghost

CAPTAIN
MATT URBAN

"**W**e're getting our butts kicked, Captain!" the frantic soldier shouted after scrambling down a hill and away from heavy German firepower during a fierce battle outside the town of Renouf, France.

Captain Matt Urban grabbed the baby-faced private Dave Russell by the arm and made him stop. "What did you see up there?"

"Two Panzers [German tanks]. They're raking our unit's positions. I saw a lot of casualties, Captain. It's bad. Very bad."

"Then we're going to have to put a stop to that, aren't we, soldier? Follow me." Urban hustled over to a supply of arms and picked up a bazooka. "Grab some ammo and come with me, Russell. We're going to take out those tanks."

"But if our men up there can't stop them, how are just the two of us going to do it?"

"I don't know. But we have to try or else we'll all end up dead."

The fighting in the French countryside had been intense ever since D-day, when the Allies invaded Normandy five days earlier. The Germans were giving up ground grudgingly and at a huge cost of American lives. Outside of Renouf, the captain's men were bogged down under enemy fire and risked getting surrounded if they couldn't destroy the German tanks.

Urban and the private sneaked through the hedgerows while the rest of the troops remained pinned down from the tanks' withering machine-gunfire. The closer Urban moved toward the tanks, the angrier he felt. *They're killing and maiming my men! This must stop now!*

His blood boiling with fury and his heart pumping from the strain of combat, Urban leaped up out of a hedgerow, rested the bazooka on his shoulder, and fired an antitank rocket. *Ka-BLAM!* The first tank shuddered and exploded in smoke. "Yes!"

After only a second's worth of self-congratulations, Urban bolted from his position to avoid return fire from the Germans. He reloaded his bazooka and jumped out into the open again. While Russell tried to give him cover, Urban paid little heed to the enemy bullets whizzing past him and fired his second rocket. It scored another direct hit. He dived for cover behind a hedgerow and then sprinted over to his troops. "All right, men!" he yelled. "Let's rout the Krauts!"

With both tanks out of commission and spurred on by their

heroic commander, the Americans rose from their defensive positions and drove the Germans out of the town.

The strong-willed mustachioed commander had been rescuing his men from possible defeat ever since his first combat experience 20 months earlier when he was a 22-year-old officer. In November 1942, his unit — Company F, Ninth Infantry Division, Second Battalion, Sixtieth Infantry Regiment — was part of the invasion of North Africa, which was then under the thumb of Nazi Germany. While his fellow soldiers boarded landing craft off the African coast, Urban had been ordered to remain aboard the troop ship to prepare entertainment for the soldiers after their return from the battle. The command infuriated him because he wanted to fight alongside his men.

Soon reports came back that his platoon was facing fierce resistance on the beach. Unwilling to remain on board any longer, Urban decided to join the soldiers. He inflated a rubber raft and was lowering it in the water, when a colonel ordered him to remain on the ship. "I can't, sir," Urban told him. "My rightful place is with my platoon. They're under siege and could use my help."

"If you leave this ship, I will have you court-martialed for disobeying orders."

"With all due respect, sir, I was trained to fight and that's what I am going to do." Boldly defying a direct command, Urban hopped into the raft and paddled to the beachside battle where he met up with his fellow troops and fought valiantly. When their platoon leader was wounded, Urban replaced him and led the men in a convincing defeat of the Germans. After the battle, Urban was not punished for his defiance. Instead he was promoted to executive officer of Company F.

By March 1943, U.S. and British forces had advanced to Tunisia, the northernmost country in Africa, where they fought the Germans. Urban knocked out an enemy observation post single-handedly and then led his company in a successful assault on a strong German position. Twice he was injured from shrapnel, once in the arm and once in the hand, but both times he refused to quit fighting until the battles were won. For his fearless exploits, he received two Silver Stars, a Bronze Star, and two Purple Hearts (one for each combat injury).

Now here he was, a little more than a year later, savoring his latest battle victory in northern France. After smashing the enemy in Renouf, Urban and his troops advanced toward the village of Orglandes.

Once again, Company F ended up pinned down by heavy artillery and tank fire. Taking a platoon with him, Urban tried to outflank the enemy. "We can do this!" he assured the men. "Let's show 'em what we've got! Let's get . . . Ahh!" Shrapnel from an exploding shell fired by a nearby Panzer tore into his left leg and sent him crashing to the ground, knocking the wind out of him.

Urban groaned from the sharp pain that made his leg feel on fire. *I've got to direct my men.* He tried crawling to a better vantage point, but he couldn't.

A medic rushed over and began treating him. "Captain, this wound looks pretty serious — a bad laceration and a possible fracture," said the medic. "We need to evacuate you to the rear."

"Nonsense!" barked Urban. "Just shoot me up with a painkiller."

"But, sir . . ."

"Shut up and do it. That's an order. I'm not leaving my men."

The medic did as he was told. Urban then regrouped his men, moving them into defensive positions for the night. Urban didn't sleep well because of the pain from his wound. But before dawn, he staggered to his feet and directed his company in a counterattack. Not one to remain in the rear, he was fighting on the front lines when a salvo of mortar rounds landed all around him. As he ducked for cover, a piece of shrapnel sliced open his left arm.

Losing blood and nearly unconscious, Urban was in no condition to command his unit. He was treated on the battlefield and then evacuated to the rear and shipped to a hospital in southern England. It was his first time away from his men, and he wasn't a good patient. Despite his serious injuries, he was raring to return to combat. "I belong on the battlefield, not in a hospital," he groused to anyone who would listen. "I'm a fighter. I've always been a fighter."

Growing up in Buffalo, New York, Urban loved to box in competition. He worked at various after-school jobs and earned enough money to attend Cornell University, where he became a collegiate boxing champion in 1939. He channeled his zeal for fighting by joining the Army and becoming an officer. For him now to be recuperating in a hospital with a bum arm and leg was incredibly frustrating, because he wanted to be with his men. But the doctors insisted he needed several more weeks of recovery before he could even think of seeing combat again.

After a month in the hospital, Urban was sitting in the hospital ward, reading a newspaper article describing the latest Allied setbacks in northern France. He slammed the paper down in disgust. "Damn those Krauts!" he snarled to no one in particular.

"Captain Urban? Is that you?" It was Private Russell, sitting in a wheelchair, his right leg in a cast and much of his head bandaged.

Leaning on a cane, Urban limped over to him. "Russell! What happened to you?"

"A grenade got me. They brought me here two days ago. They think they can save my leg, but I'll probably lose an eye."

"That's a tough break. How are the rest of my men?"

"Not so good, Captain. We've been getting beat up for weeks near Orglandes. Lots more casualties. You wouldn't recognize the guys. You know how you always told us we were a first-class fighting machine? Well, Company F is broken down. They're frightened and discouraged. Morale is lower than a bomb crater."

The news made Urban sick to his stomach. *My men aren't quitters. Something's wrong, terribly wrong. They're good soldiers. What they need is some strong leadership, that's all. They need someone with battle experience to inspire them and lead them. They need someone like . . . me.*

"Russell, take care of yourself. I've got to go."

"Where, Captain?"

"Back to where I belong."

Urban knew the doctors wouldn't release him anytime soon, so he decided to slip out of the hospital. After the nurse put fresh bandages on his wounded leg and arm, Urban dressed in his fatigues and told the hospital staff, "I'm going to sit outside for a while and get some fresh air."

He hobbled on his cane out the front door and talked a private into giving him a ride to the nearby air base. From there, Urban hopped on a military plane to France and then spent four days hitchhiking on Army trucks and jeeps. He arrived July 25 at the Second Battalion command post near the front lines and learned that Company F had left a half hour earlier for the village of Saint-Lô as part of an attack called Operation Cobra. One of the battalion officers told him, "I don't know how well they'll perform. They're pretty banged up. They're so worn out it's as if they have no more fight left in them."

"Oh, they still have plenty of fight in them," Urban insisted. "They just need me to show them where to look."

Fired up by his anger at the Germans and despair over the fate of his men, Urban ordered a private to drive him to Saint-Lô. A short while later, they approached the rear of an intense battle. His men looked tired and timid, not anything like the bold and daring troops he had led the previous month. Urban got out of the jeep and told the acting company commander, "I'm retaking command of Company F." Then, with one hand waving a pistol and the other gripping his cane, Urban limped toward his men, growling like a tiger. "Come on, men! It's time we turned those Krauts into sauerkraut. We're gonna kick them outta here, and I'm gonna lead the way!"

The sight of their wounded commander hobbling down the road, itching to fight, instantly boosted the low morale of his troops. Encouraged by the surprise return of their leader, the men found their second wind and regained their confidence. Following his directions, they attacked the Germans.

Rattling off orders, moving soldiers, and firing his own weapon, Urban guided his troops as they pushed back the enemy. But as dusk settled in, Company F's surge stalled under scathing machine-gunfire from a well-entrenched German position atop a prominent hill. Two of the three Allied tanks that had been the Americans' main firepower had been destroyed. The third tank, which was partway up the hill, was intact but not moving, because its driver and gunner had been killed.

Urban collared a sergeant and the lieutenant in charge of the tanks and created a plan of attack. The two soldiers needed to run out into the open for 100 yards, get into the tank, and take out the German position on the hill if the Americans were to advance. Urban and his troops laid down cover for the lieutenant and sergeant during their mad dash in the open. They made it to the tank safely, but while climbing aboard, the two men were cut down by machine-gunfire.

As tough as Urban was, he couldn't stop the tears from welling up. *I just ordered them to their deaths. It's almost suicidal to try it again, but we must. I can't ask two more to sacrifice their lives. But I know of one who is willing.*

He dropped his cane, turned to the men nearest him, and said, "Cover me."

"But, Captain," said a sergeant, "you're in no condition . . ."

"Cover me!" Urban snapped. As he crawled out from behind a hedge, he told the sergeant, "If I make it, bring my cane with you. If I don't make it, tell my wife I love her." He brushed off the pain in his injured arm and leg and crawled along the grass toward the tank. His men directed fire at the Germans in an effort to draw attention away from Urban. *I know this is foolish and I'm headed for certain death, but I have to try. If the Krauts spot me, they'll turn me into Swiss cheese.* Those 100 yards seemed so far, far away.

When Urban was halfway to the tank, a German noticed him and began shooting. "Damn!" Urban got up and half ran, half hobbled toward the tank, snaking his way as bullets nipped at his feet. He expected at any moment to get shot. Incredibly, he made it to the tank and, with machine-gun bullets ricocheting around him, mounted the turret and climbed in. *I made it! I can't believe it!*

After catching his breath, he opened the top hatch, exposing his head, and gripped the tank's .50-caliber machine gun. Spraying a deadly stream of fire, Urban mowed down the Germans as his troops, buoyed by his courageous efforts, charged the enemy position and wiped it out, completely turning the tide of the battle to their favor.

The next morning, during a lull, Urban was drinking a hot cup of coffee when the sergeant came up to him and said, "I have something for you, Captain." He handed Urban his cane. "But then, the way you were hustling toward that tank, maybe you don't need it."

Urban smiled and took the cane. He still needed it because his actions had opened up the wound in his leg.

Day after day, Company F — now fighting with renewed vigor — and the rest of the battalion steadily advanced, driving the Germans back. But each battle proved brutal. Within a week after his arrival, Urban threw away his cane and limped without it, even though the constant pain reminded him that he wasn't fully recovered.

On August 2, a week after his return, Urban was leading a charge when a mortar round exploded a few yards away from him. Flying pieces of shell fragments sliced into his chest, knocking him hard on his back. His fellow soldiers dragged him to the rear of the lines where medics pulled out the shrapnel and sewed him up. The battalion surgeon told Urban, "Your wounds are serious, and you should be evacuated. You need time to recover."

"Nonsense," Urban said. "I've been nicked up a little bit, but I'm better off here than in a hospital. Case closed."

Four days later, the battalion commander was seriously wounded. Although there were other officers older and higher in rank than Urban, the Army promoted him to command the Second Battalion because of his extraordinary combat exploits.

On August 15, he was issuing orders along the front lines when he suffered another wound — his fourth since arriving in France — this time from shrapnel from a grenade that tore into his back. The battalion surgeon knew better than to suggest that Urban recuperate in a hospital. Instead, the doctor removed the shrapnel and stitched up the captain's back.

To his men, Urban seemed indestructible. Bullets and shrapnel from a tank gun, grenade, and mortar hadn't stopped him. His resolve was so powerful that it rubbed off on his men who were once again the mean green fighting machine. They had shoved the enemy across northern France back to the border of German-held Belgium and had taken dozens of prisoners.

On September 3, the Second Battalion was given the mission of establishing a safe spot where troops and supplies could cross the Meuse River near Heer, Belgium. However, when the Americans reached the river, they discovered the Germans had concentrated forces at the Meuse. Fierce enemy artillery, small arms, and mortar fire thwarted the battalion's attack. Realizing the mission was in jeopardy, Urban left his command post and moved to the front lines, where he reorganized the troops and personally led a charge toward the enemy's strongpoint.

As the attack moved across an open field laced with machine-gunfire, Urban, running with a bad limp, suddenly clutched his throat and fell to the ground. A bullet had drilled into his neck, through his windpipe, and flew out the other side. His mind reeling, Urban kept his shaky hands on his throat while he gasped for breath and coughed up blood. He was afraid that if he let go of his throat, the blood would gush out. *Is this it?* he wondered. *Is this how I die?* Then he passed out.

A medic rushed to the captain's side, stopped the bleeding, and put a tube down his throat, so Urban could breathe. Then litter bearers rushed the wounded captain off the battlefield. Back in the rear, he regained consciousness. *I'm still here.*

He looked up and saw a priest, who was a military chaplain, leaning over him, praying, and giving him last rites. *I must be dying.* Urban tried to sit up but was too woozy. Seeing the battalion surgeon arrive, Urban tried to talk but could only make a garbled whisper. "It's . . . that . . . bad?"

"We need to evacuate you immediately," the doctor replied. "You've suffered a life-threatening injury."

Urban shook his head. Weakly gripping the doctor's hand, he whispered haltingly, "I stay here . . . until the mission . . . is accomplished."

Although in horrible pain and trying to remain conscious, Urban jotted down a new attack plan on a piece of paper and handed it to the sergeant to give to the acting commander. Not until late in the day, when he heard from an officer that the Americans had secured the river crossing-point, did the captain agree to be evacuated.

As Urban was put in an ambulance that would take him to a docked hospital ship, one of his soldiers came over to him and said, "Good luck, Captain, or should I say *der Geist*?"

"What . . . does . . . that . . . mean?" Urban whispered.

"That's German for 'The Ghost.' The prisoners told us that's what the Germans call you, because every time they think they've killed you, you show up to fight them again."

While Urban was on a hospital ship headed for England, all the men of Company F were either killed in action or taken prisoner. Among the dead was a battalion officer who had written up a recommendation that Urban receive the Medal of Honor. The letter, which Urban knew nothing about, got lost in Army bureaucracy.

Even without such an honor, Urban, who was given a medical discharge in 1946 and retired as a lieutenant colonel, became one of most decorated soldiers in American history. He earned more than two dozen combat medals, including a Purple Heart with six oak leaf clusters, representing the seven times he was injured.

It took more than 35 years before the long-lost recommendation was discovered, triggering an examination of his records and interviews with surviving members of his unit. When the truth became known how the brave captain had risked his life time and again to save his men, the Army realized he deserved the medal. In 1980, President Jimmy Carter presented Urban with the Medal of Honor, calling him "the greatest soldier in our country's history."

Urban never fully recovered from his wounds. Because the bullet had damaged his vocal cords, he could talk only in a raspy voice for the rest of his life. After the war, he moved with his wife and daughter to Michigan where at different times he headed the parks and recreation departments of Port Huron, Monroe, and Holland.

Matt Urban died in 1995 in Holland, Michigan, from complications caused by his many war wounds. He was 75. He is buried in Arlington National Cemetery alongside so many other courageous soldiers who fought for America's freedom.

From Jerk to Hero

SERGEANT
MAYNARD "SNUFFY" SMITH

With his uniform shirt untucked and his shoes unpolished, Sergeant Maynard Smith scowled while the much younger lieutenant chewed him out.

"Sergeant, you look like a sad sack," scolded the officer. "Tuck in your shirt and polish your boots. This is the Army Air Corps, not a gang of punks."

Smith rolled his eyes and hissed, "Oh, spare me, Lieutenant. The way I look doesn't mean a hill of beans when it comes to war."

"You're wrong. Taking pride in your appearance means taking pride in everything else you do — including fighting."

The 32-year-old sergeant shook his head and sneered, "I was riding Harleys when you were still on a tricycle. I don't need to listen to you." Then he stormed off.

For that show of defiance, Smith was given KP duty — which meant he spent the next week on "kitchen police," peeling potatoes and cleaning out garbage cans in the mess hall at his air base in Thurleigh, England.

Ever since his arrival in April 1943, Smith never seemed to fit in. His stubborn temperament, obnoxious personality, and know-it-all attitude had made him the most despised man on the base. For a little guy who was only five feet five inches tall and weighed 130 pounds, he had a chip on his shoulder the size of a cement block. Smith especially hated taking orders from officers who were 10 years younger than him. Time and again, he shirked his duties and ignored authority. As a result, he was often punished with extra KP duty and wasn't allowed to fly, even though he was trained as a ball-turret gunner on the B-17 bomber.

He had come from money — his father was a wealthy judge in Michigan — but Smith had shown little ambition and a bad attitude throughout his 20s and into his 30s. When he got in trouble with the law, he was given two choices — go to jail or enlist in the military. He chose to join the Army Air Corps.

His reputation as a jerk spread quickly at Thurleigh. Soon his fellow airmen at the 423rd Squadron, 306th Bomb Group, Eighth Air Force mocked Smith by giving him the nickname Snuffy after a popular comic-strip character, the ornery mountain man Snuffy Smith.

"Usually new arrivals are immediately assigned to a crew to replace a man who was killed or wounded," Lieutenant Lewis P. Johnson, a B-17 pilot, told Smith one day. "Didn't you ever wonder why you've been here for six weeks and haven't flown yet?"

Smith's response was a glare and a grunt.

"It's because no one wants to fly with you, Snuffy," Johnson said. "You're a pompous jerk and not a team player. You don't seem to care about anything. No one likes you."

"Since when is being popular a requirement for being a good airman?" Smith countered.

"It isn't. But being a team player and doing your job to the best of your ability are requirements."

"Why are you giving me this boring lecture, Lieutenant?"

"Because you've been assigned to my bomber for a mission tomorrow. Look, Snuffy, my crew is a tight-knit veteran group. We've successfully gone through many dangerous flights together because we get along so well. Now we're stuck with you as our ball-turret gunner. Our lives depend on teamwork, and now you're part of that team. Even though you're a jerk, you'd better come through or we all could die, including you."

Johnson, who towered over the short sergeant, leaned down, looked him straight in the eyes, and said, "I don't intend to die. This will be my twenty-fifth mission. That means I get to go home after its successful completion. I won't let you screw this up."

Smith smiled and said, "Relax, sir. Even jerks can become heroes."

The next morning, nearly 30 B-17s were getting ready to take off from Thurleigh. Their objective: Bomb the submarine pens — concrete bunkers in harbors where German U-boats were manufactured or repaired — at Nazi-occupied Saint-Nazaire, France. The American airmen called the town Flak City because it was defended by a huge number of antiaircraft batteries. Raids to Saint-Nazaire were among the most deadly for the Eighth Air Force because only half the planes ever returned safely.

Radioman Henry Bean wagged his finger at Smith and said, "This will be my twenty-first mission. I need to complete four more before I can go home. You better do your job — and do it well."

"Just worry about yourself," Smith retorted. After the plane reached cruising altitude, Smith lowered himself into the small Plexiglas bubble under the bomber, where he would be responsible for defending the B-17's belly against German fighter planes.

Despite his cocky attitude, Smith was nervous during the flight but didn't show it. As the bombers neared Saint-Nazaire, flak dotted the sky. He watched in eerie fascination the black puffs of smoke and noticed tiny bits of shrapnel harmlessly strike the turret. Over the interphone, he heard the bombardier declare, "Bombs away!"

"We're heading home," Johnson announced to the crew. "No Jerries [Germans] in sight. It's been such a smooth mission I ought to ditch this plane just off the coast so I'll have a dramatic story to tell my children someday," he joked.

Minutes later, the returning bombers descended to 2,000 feet as they approached what Smith assumed was the coastline of Great Britain. *Well, this was an easy mission,* he told himself. Patting his two .50-caliber machine guns, he thought, *I didn't even get to fire my twin fifties.*

Unknown to almost everyone, the lead navigator had miscalculated the flight home. Instead of crossing the English coast, the bombers were flying directly over the German-occupied city of Brest, France. Smith, like the rest of the crew, was shocked by sudden deadly antiaircraft fire now blotting the sky.

From inside the Plexiglas turret, he gasped when he saw a Flying Fortress take a direct hit and fall in a trail of smoke and fire. *That could have been us,* he thought. *Will the next shell hit us? I wish we were already back in England.*

He gulped after spotting the first wave of enemy fighters zooming toward the bombers. Another B-17 exploded in midair, this time by cannon fire from one of the attackers.

His stomach twisted in knots, Smith thought, *Be alert or be dead.* His bomber headed out over the English Channel when German fighters from the left and right side began raking the plane with a flurry of bullets. As the B-17 shuddered from the onslaught, Smith and the other gunners onboard unleashed their own firepower. From below and above, the swarm of fighters attacked with a fury. Everywhere he looked, Smith saw an enemy plane. With clenched teeth, he kept up a steady stream of fire below him, then off to the right, then straight ahead.

Out of the corner of his eye, he saw tracer bullets from one of the fighters close in on the plane. A deafening explosion rocked the B-17. *We've been hit!* He could see smoke swirling from the left wing. "How bad is it?" he asked in the interphone.

No response. He figured the communication system had been knocked out. And judging by the way the engines were sputtering, he knew the plane wasn't flying well.

Smith needed to focus on the German fighters that were coming in for the kill. He kept firing at them until the electrical controls that allowed him to maneuver his guns in the turret had been shot out. *My guns are all but useless now,* he thought. *I'm a sitting duck if I stay here. I need to see what's going on in the fuselage.*

He climbed out of the turret and opened an armored hatch into the midsection of the plane. "Oh, damn!" he shouted. Flames were shooting out from the radio room ahead of him, and another fire was smoldering in the tail section behind him.

"Flak hit the fuel tanks on the left wing and ruptured them!" yelled Bean, the radioman. "Fuel poured into the radio room and caught fire, and now the five of us on this side of the fire are trapped."

"What about the cockpit?" asked Smith. In the front of the plane, on the other side of the fire, were the pilot, copilot, navigator, bombardier, and flight engineer.

"All our communications are knocked out, but I think the crew up there are all right, because we're still flying. [Flight engineer Bill] Fahrenhold yelled back to us that some of the control cables had been shot out. The plane is a flying wreck. We're doomed. There's no way we can make it home."

"We can't just stand around here," Smith declared. "We've got to do something."

"You're right. I know what I'm going to do," said Bean, adjusting the straps of the parachute on his back. He pushed

Smith aside an d made a beeline for the open gun hatch and dived out.

The bomber's veteran waist gunners, Joseph Bukacek and Robert Folliard, decided to follow Bean's lead. Bukacek jumped out next. But when Folliard tried, he got hung up half in and half out of the gun hatch, because his parachute pack was snagged on the barrel of a machine gun. "Help me! Help me!" he screamed.

Smith yanked him back into the burning fuselage and said, "Stay here and help me put out the fire."

"It's no use!" shouted Folliard, pushing him away. "I'm getting out of here!"

"All right, but let me help you bail out." Smith opened the rear escape door and watched Folliard jump out and clear the burning plane. His parachute opened seconds later.

Should I jump, too? Smith wondered. *If I do, there will be no one left to fight the fire. It'll burn up the plane until it breaks apart. The others up front won't stand a chance.* In his 32 years of life, Smith never really thought about anyone other than himself. He had always looked out only for number one. But this time, with the fate of the bomber and the remaining crewmen in his hands, a new feeling crept over him — the need to help others even at the risk of his own safety. He blocked out any further thoughts of bailing out and made up his mind to try to save the plane and the rest of the crew.

Smith gagged from the thick smoke and the smell of fuel that was rapidly filling up the fuselage. He wrapped a scarf around his face so it would act like an air filter. Then he grabbed a fire extinguisher and attacked the fire in the radio room.

Glancing over his shoulder at the other, smaller fire behind him, he spotted tail gunner Roy Gibson on his hands and knees crawling through the flames. He was covered with blood.

"I've . . . been . . . hit," Gibson wheezed before collapsing.

Smith dragged Gibson away from the flames and quickly examined him. Either a bullet or a piece of shrapnel had struck the tail gunner in the chest, piercing his left lung. Smith rolled the wounded man onto his left side to keep blood from filling the right lung and suffocating him.

"Trouble . . . breathing . . . Oh . . . the pain." Gibson began thrashing around from his agony. Then he clutched Smith by the collar of his jacket and muttered, "I'm . . . dying."

"Yeah, you probably are, but I'm going to help you anyway." Pulling out a first-aid kit, Smith bandaged the wound and gave Gibson an injection of morphine that eased the pain and calmed him. Smith then returned to fight the blazes.

While frantically trying to snuff out the flames, he heard bullets slamming into the side of the plane. He peeked out the side hatch and shouted, "Not again!"

Enemy fighters were still attacking the bombers. Out the side hatch, he saw a German plane lining up for another deadly pass at the floundering B-17. Smith dropped his fire extinguisher, raced to the left waist gun, and shot at the fighter. As the enemy plane passed beneath the burning bomber, Smith switched to the right waist gun to deliver a parting series of .50-caliber rounds. *Missed him! But I bet I scared the hell out of him. He won't come back — I hope.*

Returning to the radio room where the blaze was at its worst, Smith was stunned by what he saw. The intense heat had not only melted the wires, the radio, and other equipment, but also had burned gaping holes right through the fuselage. "I don't believe it," he said out loud. Between the flames, he could see the whitecaps of the English Channel below. *How much longer before the plane burns up or breaks up?*

Smith concentrated on saving the plane. *I've got to starve the fire by getting rid of anything that can burn.* He began tossing flaming debris through the hatches to clear the area of anything flammable.

Suddenly, more bullets whizzed past him. *They're coming from inside the plane. What's going on?* Then he figured it out. Flames had reached an ammunition belt, causing the bullets to explode from the fire. He took cover until the fire had consumed those bullets. Then he tossed out other boxes of ammo belts, too, before they blew up.

I'd better keep some ammo with me just in case. Looking out the hatch, he grimaced, because the Germans weren't giving up their assault. *Damn, they didn't leave like I thought.* Manning the left waist gun again, he fired a burst, driving off a German pilot. Then he ran back to the radio room and continued to battle the fire until he used up the last of the fluid in the extinguisher. In desperation, he poured out the contents of a few water bottles and urine buckets on the flames.

Above the noise of the wind whistling through the holes of the plane and of the machine-gunfire, Smith heard Gibson scream out in agony. Smith returned to the tail gunner, who muttered, "I can't . . . stand . . . the pain." *Now what am I going to do?* Smith gave Gibson another injection of morphine and told him, "Don't die on me. We're nearing the coast of England." Gibson slipped back into unconsciousness from the shot.

More bullets struck the plane. *Don't those Jerries ever give up?* Smith hurried to the left waist gun, looked out, and saw that a lone German fighter had turned around for another attack. Once again, Smith manned the machine gun and fired several rounds, forcing the fighter to veer off.

Smith looked down at his ammo belt. He had run out of bullets. *If the Jerry makes another pass, there's no way I can defend the bomber.* Fortunately, the fighter, like most of the German pursuit planes, had limited fuel, and flew away.

Smith returned to the burned radio room, whipped off his sweater, and used it to beat out the last of the flames. He ran to the tail section and stomped on the smaller blaze, snuffing it out as his shoes and clothes began to smolder.

For 90 tense minutes, Smith had been hustling between the two fires, tending to Gibson, and shooting at the German fighters. Now he was running out of gas emotionally and physically. *I just want to get this over with and go home.* He slumped on the floor, hoping that the pilot and copilot could bring in the crippled craft safely.

Smith knew the odds were stacked against them. The plane had been riddled with bullets, the fire had burned holes in the fuselage, and the engines were coughing and nearly out of fuel. *Can this plane hold together long enough for us to land?*

Fearing that the heat had weakened the B-17's fuselage, Smith had a sudden thought. *I need to lighten the load.* He jumped to his feet and began throwing out everything in the rear of the plane that wasn't too hot, too heavy, or bolted down.

Just then, flight engineer Bill Fahrenhold worked his way to the midsection of the plane. "Is everyone okay here?"

"Bukacek, Folliard, and Bean bailed out. Gibson is in terrible shape with a bullet wound through his lung. This plane is ready to fall apart any second. I assume Johnson is still flying the plane."

"Yeah. He and the others are okay. We're going to land at the first available airfield in a few minutes. I don't know if the plane can handle the stress of a landing. Just be prepared. Can you take care of Gibson?"

"Yeah, I'll make sure he gets off if we crash. Tell Johnson that any pilot worth his salt should be able to put this baby on the ground in one piece."

Fahrenhold ignored the remark. "I'll warn you when we're about fifty feet from touchdown."

The B-17 sputtered and shook as it descended toward an airfield at Predannack, Cornwall, England. Smith looked at Gibson, who was groaning. "We're almost there," said Smith. "You better not die on me, okay? Or I'm going to be royally ticked off."

"Fifty feet!" Fahrenhold shouted to Smith.

Nursing a lumbering, shot-up plane, Johnson gently brought the bomber onto the runway as the wheels gave a slight squeal. *Not bad,* thought Smith. But when the tail wheel hit the ground, the stress was too much for the bomber. The fuselage folded, splitting open at the radio room. The two sections skidded and bumped down the runway while Smith held on to Gibson. When the remains of the broken plane screeched to a halt, Smith hopped out and yelled for medics to get Gibson off on a stretcher. The rest of the crew scrambled out of the nose, which had been shattered by flak.

As the airmen walked away from the wreck, Johnson went up to Smith and said, "Good job back there. You saved our lives."

"I'm not such a bad airman after all, am I?"

Johnson nodded and then with a straight face added, "But you're still a jerk."

Later that day, Smith was sitting alone outside the barracks when Fahrenhold showed up and said, "Guess how many bullet and shrapnel holes our B-17 took."

"About two thousand," Smith replied.

"Wrong. Try three thousand five hundred."

"And the plane still flew," marveled Smith. "We should take our hats off to the people who built it."

"Gee, Snuffy. That's the first nice thing I've ever heard you say about anyone."

The three crewmen who had bailed out were never found. Of the 29 B-17s that took part in the May 1, 1943, mission to Saint-Nazaire, seven never came home. The toll: 75 airmen dead or missing, and 15 wounded.

Johnson told his superiors about Smith's heroics and wrote up a recommendation for the Medal of Honor. Although recognized as a hero, Smith still didn't make any new friends, and he still frustrated his superior officers with his lack of military discipline. But in the air, he remained all business.

After returning from his fourth mission, Smith was ordered to see the commanding officer. *I wonder what trouble I'm in now*, he thought.

When he arrived, he was surprised to see that the CO [commanding officer] was smiling. "Congratulations, Sergeant. The military brass has approved the Medal of Honor for you. And get this: It will be presented by none other than the Secretary of War himself, Henry Stimson."

As a reward, Smith was given a pass, allowing him to go into the nearby town and celebrate. Unfortunately, he partied a little too long and returned to the base so late that he missed an important briefing. Another turret gunner was forced to take his place on a mission that Smith was supposed to be on.

As a result, Smith was ordered to see the commanding officer again. This time, when Smith arrived, the CO was not smiling. "You messed up again, Sergeant. You've shown complete irresponsibility. You're on KP for the rest of the week."

Meanwhile, the base cleaned up the parade grounds in preparation for the Medal of Honor presentation, which turned into a major event. On the day of the ceremony, Eighth Air Force commander General Ira C. Eaker, six other generals, and the Secretary of War arrived. Also showing up were several reporters, photographers, and two radio correspondents ready to broadcast the event live to the United States. The band was assembled, the bombers were prepared for their flyover, sound systems were set up and checked, and the troops were lined up.

Everything was ready — until someone asked, "Where's Snuffy?"

Several airmen scurried around the base in search of the missing hero. They finally found him — on KP duty scraping leftovers from the metal breakfast trays.

On orders from the commanding officer, Smith quickly cleaned himself up, dressed in a crisp uniform, and hurried to the ceremony.

After the band played, General Eaker announced, "Sergeant Smith not only performed his duty, he carried on after others more experienced than he was had given up. Through his presence of mind, determination, and bravery, he saved himself and the lives of six of his crewmates and the Fortress in which they all flew."

Secretary of War Stimson then placed the Medal of Honor around Smith's neck while the generals saluted him. Smith stepped to the microphone. Here was his chance to say whatever he wanted, to tell the world about his heroics. Into the mike, he said, "Thank you." And nothing more.

Maynard "Snuffy" Smith was the first enlisted airman to earn the Medal of Honor. Eventually, because of disciplinary problems and his disdain for the military life, he was busted to private and given an honorable discharge in 1945. Hailed as a hero in his hometown of Caro, Michigan, Smith never found much success either in marriage or business. He died in 1984, six days before his seventy-third birthday.

Buffalo Soldier

SECOND LIEUTENANT
VERNON BAKER

Twenty-two-year-old Vernon Baker wanted something more out of life. As a young African-American man in Cheyenne, Wyoming — a town with only a dozen other black families — his options were limited. It was 1941, a time when the fabric of the United States had been stained by racism. And yet Baker wanted to serve his country in the military.

He walked into an Army recruiting office, where a scowling sergeant was sitting behind the desk, reading a magazine, and deliberately ignoring him for several minutes. Finally, the sergeant looked up and snarled, "What do *you* want?"

"I want to enlist in the Army," Baker replied.

"We don't have any need for people like you," sneered the sergeant. Then he returned to his reading, pretending that Baker was no longer there.

Baker seethed, but kept his anger in check. As he headed out the door, he glanced at the recruiting poster on the wall. Uncle Sam was pointing and saying, "I WANT YOU!" The irony didn't escape him.

Orphaned at age four when his parents were killed in a car accident, Baker was raised by his grandparents in their boardinghouse in Cheyenne. He spent two years at Father Flanagan's Boys Home in Omaha, Nebraska, and graduated from high school in Iowa. He worked as a railroad porter and a shoe-shine boy. But that kind of life held no future for him. He was determined to join the Army.

He swallowed his pride and returned to the recruiting office. His gut was twisting with the thought of facing that bigot again. But this time, a different sergeant was sitting behind the desk. "Can I help you?" the recruiter asked politely.

"Yes, I'd like to enlist in the Army," Baker answered.

"Fine, son. Pull up a chair and let's see if I can help you out."

Baker soon was a member of the U.S. Army — a segregated army, which he was reminded of time and again. Days after he enlisted, Baker stepped off the train in Mineral Wells, Texas, and boarded a bus for Camp Wolters for basic training. He sat down in the seat directly behind the driver. In a split second, the driver wheeled around and roared, "Get up and get to the back of the bus where you belong!"

Baker shot up and clenched his fists, ready to swing, but an older black man rushed forward and grabbed him by the collar. "You planning to die on your first day in Texas?" he drawled. "In case you haven't noticed, you're a colored man. Colored folks can't sit anywhere they please in the South.

Nobody here would try to sit up front unless he wanted to get killed."

The resentment Baker felt because of prejudice against his race intensified during his early army days. After basic training, he transferred to Fort Huachuca, Arizona, where he was made the company clerk because he could read, write, and type. Soon after the United States entered the war, he was promoted to staff sergeant.

At the fort, many white soldiers had spent 20 years as privates and corporals without being promoted, because they couldn't read or write. They resented high-school graduates who were promoted over them. Seeing a black man with all those stripes infuriated them. One night, as Baker was returning to his quarters, three white veteran corporals surrounded him. "What we got here is a real smart black boy," growled one sarcastically. Then they pounced on him, punching him in the head and stomach until he was a bloody mess. Leaving him sprawled on the ground, they chortled, "Yeah, that's one smart black boy."

Baker kept the assault to himself. He knew that if he reported it, he faced retaliation. Once again, he swallowed his pride and kept his temper in check. It wasn't easy, but he remembered something his grandfather always told him: "Don't hate. Because if you hate, it will destroy you."

Baker eventually went to officer candidates' school, where blacks ate and slept in their own barracks and joined the whites only in class. He passed with flying colors and was commissioned a second lieutenant on January 11, 1943. He was assigned to the 370th Regiment, Ninety-second Infantry, an all-black division known as the Buffalo Soldiers. The name originally had been given to black soldiers a century earlier during the Indian wars.

"You know why we call you that?" Baker's white commander said. "It's because you boys' black skin and nappy hair remind us of buffaloes." The commander added that the War Department had decided that all black combat troops had to be led by white southerners "because we know best how to handle you people."

One day during the summer, all the officers were called to division headquarters. Even though Baker was an officer, he and the other black officers always had to enter through the back door, while the white officers came in the front. But on this day, the black officers weren't allowed inside at all and were told to sit under a nearby tree. Later the chief of staff came out and told them, "The division is going to ship out soon. All the white boys have been going overseas, and now it's time for you black boys to go get killed." He flashed a sinister grin.

The resentment that Baker and his black comrades felt was tempered by their anticipation of finally seeing combat. From the moment the United States was attacked at Pearl Harbor, the black soldiers yearned to fight the enemy even if it meant joining a force filled with racists. Baker knew firsthand his homeland was imperfect, but he believed it was still the best country in the world.

The Buffalo Soldiers were sent to Italy to help drive out the German troops who occupied the country. As their ship crossed the Atlantic, Baker realized that most of the men couldn't read or write, so he wrote letters home for them. Once the men reached Italy, they marched north toward the towns of Pisa and Lucca and the front lines.

Despite white officers' mistaken belief that blacks couldn't fight at night, the blacks' first four months in combat were spent on effective night patrols that often led to skirmishes with Germans. In one of the encounters, Baker was shot in the wrist and needed surgery to repair it.

He tried to look out for his men, encouraging them to fight for America and not for the southern white colonels and generals who considered black soldiers inferior, no matter how well the African-Americans completed their missions. "It's difficult to tell who the bigger racists are — the commanders behind us or the Germans in front of us," he admitted to the men of his platoon.

The enemy fortifications seemed impossible to breach up and down the Gothic Line, a 200-mile-wide defense along mountain ridgelines. The Gothic Line guarded all the routes to northern Italy and prevented any advance into the Po Valley, an agricultural and manufacturing area vital to supporting the Nazi war machine. Huge German guns protected exposed slopes and were aimed straight down roads, ravines, and gullies. Built in the sides of the mountains were thousands of bunkers, machine-gun nests, and observation posts. They were all reinforced with rocks, logs, railroad ties, and several feet of dirt, and they blended with the rocky terrain to provide excellent camouflage.

The Ninety-second Division's objective: Castle Aghinolfi, a massive stone fortress that sat atop a mountain on the western edge of the Gothic Line. Originally built in the fifth century A.D., the fort was surrounded by rock walls, barbed wire, minefields, and a chain of howitzers, mortars, and other artillery. From every direction, the Germans could see and then bombard any advancing armies.

The only possible way to attack was by sending the infantry up a trio of terraced mountains — which the Allies named Hills X, Y, and Z — that led to the castle from the south. Early in 1945, the Allies made three attempts to capture the castle, but failed each time when German guns shelled them into oblivion.

Baker was told that his unit, Company C, would lead the next charge for Castle Aghinolfi. In the predawn hours of April 5, 1945, he donned his best, freshly cleaned uniform. *If this is going to be my last day on earth, I want to go out looking sharp,* he thought. He strapped two bandoliers of ammunition around his waist and clipped four grenades on his belt webbing. Then he clutched his trusty M-1 rifle. He left his helmet behind because he found it too cumbersome and instead wore a stocking cap.

Baker was in charge of a shorthanded weapons platoon of 26 black men who carried either .30-caliber machine guns or 60-mm mortar tubes and mortar rounds. "Men, today we're going to do it," he declared. "We're going to capture that castle." The men nodded.

At 4:45 A.M., Allied artillery — including tanks, howitzers, and long-range guns from British battleships — blasted the sides of the mountain. Baker and his soldiers, who were part of a much larger assault force, ran in the darkness across exposed countryside and then headed up Hill X, a half mile away. As they advanced, he snipped German communication lines that were strung along the hill.

Baker kept scanning the area, side to side, front to rear. Then he spotted two German machine gunners. He raised his rifle and squeezed off two rounds. Both men fell dead. He ditched their weapon and replaced it with one from his platoon manned by two of his soldiers.

A few hundred yards farther, Baker shot and killed two more enemy machine gunners and replaced them with his men. Sneaking across the hill, he spotted two tubes poking out of a slit. *Gun barrels in a camouflaged bunker.* He crawled on his belly until he was at the edge of the bunker. *One . . . two . . . three . . . here I go!* He leaped up, stuck the barrel of his gun inside the slit, and began firing as fast as he could. Then he jumped to the side and put a fresh clip in his weapon. He waited for return fire. There wasn't any. He moved to the bunker and peered inside. One German was dead. The other was still alive and reaching for a stash of grenades in the corner. Baker yanked a grenade off his belt, pulled the pin, and threw it into the bunker. It exploded in a spray of dirt, logs, and rocks.

He discovered that the bunker was not a machine-gun nest but an observation post. He cut the communications wire and returned to his men. They continued toward the next terrace when, not more than 50 feet ahead of him, he spotted another hidden machine-gun nest. *Too late. They're going to kill me!* He started shooting in the slit and was relieved when they didn't fire back. When he looked inside, he saw two dead Germans. At the moment he killed them, they had been eating their breakfast rather than keeping an eye on any invaders. *Lucky break.*

In the first two hours of the assault, Baker had brought his platoon three miles inside enemy lines and had single-handedly destroyed three machine-gun nests and an observation post and cut communication lines. *This is going better than I ever imagined.*

By 7 A.M., Baker and his men were at the edge of a rocky clearing that sloped up toward the walls of the castle. *There's no way we can rush the castle without getting picked off,* he thought. *But orders are orders. It's the only way.*

Meeting with his company commander, who was a white captain, Baker ordered his machine gunners to provide covering fire for the castle assault. As he and the captain were talking, they spotted a German flinging a grenade at them. The captain yelped and took off running, knocking Baker's gun barrel. By the time Baker could take aim, the grenade had landed five feet from him. Thinking he was about to die, Baker shot and killed the soldier as a final act of defiance. Incredibly, the grenade did not explode. *Lady Luck, thank you. Please stay with me.*

Baker carefully followed the trail the German had been on and discovered that it ended at another observation post. He tossed in two more grenades, killing another four Germans. Then he raced back toward his men. By now, the Germans were launching a salvo of mortar rounds at the Americans, killing and wounding several of them.

Second Lieutenant Walker, whose job was directing Allied

artillery fire, was on the radiophone, giving coordinates to officers miles away. He was getting frustrated. "Baker, they don't believe we could've made it this far behind enemy lines!"

Baker grabbed the phone and told the officer on the other end, "Look, we're one hundred and fifty yards south of the castle, and we're getting pounded by mortar rounds! We desperately need artillery fire on the German mortar positions. Now! Our medics can't get to the wounded and . . ." He looked up. About a dozen mortar rounds were flying toward them.

"Cover!" he yelled. Everyone dived to the ground. *Ka-boom! Ka-boom! Ka-boom!* The earth shook and men screamed. Then machine-gunfire erupted from the castle, prompting Baker to shout, "Move, men! Keep moving or die!" The soldiers who hadn't been killed or wounded hurriedly backtracked a few hundred yards away behind several boulders. They sat tight as Allied artillery finally skimmed in low over their heads and smashed into the enemy positions.

The hill rocked in pandemonium from German mortar explosions, howling Allied artillery shells, and the wails and groans of the wounded. The air blanketed the combatants with dust, debris, and the bitter smell of explosives.

During a break in the action, Baker found the captain in a nearby stone house, sitting on the dirt floor, his arms wrapped around his legs. He was pale from fright. Seeing Baker, the captain tried to hide his fear and griped, "Your men are scattered all over the place. Can't you keep them together?"

He's criticizing me while he's cowering in the corner? "I'm doing the best I can, Captain. I'll get them ready for the assault."

"You actually want to stay and fight here?"

"Yes, Captain, we can do this. We can take this castle." Looking into his terrified eyes, Baker figured the captain thought it was suicidal to try.

"Okay, you stay with your men," said the captain. "I'll go back for reinforcements."

"Right, Captain." Baker was filled with disgust. In most cases during combat, the company commander was supposed to remain on the battlefield with his men and send a soldier for reinforcements. *The captain has been running ever since that German tossed a grenade at us. He's nothing but a chicken who cares only for himself.*

After the captain left, Baker and his remaining men gathered rifles and ammo from their dead comrades. But the hardest job for him was slipping the dog tags off the bodies. He stared at each one and thanked him. Some of their faces showed terror, others pain. *These men battled to the death; God bless them.*

Baker and the survivors then hid in a slight depression on the hill and waited for the reinforcements. Suddenly, they were attacked again by mortars and heavy machine-gunfire. The Americans fought valiantly and kept the enemy at bay. All the while, Baker was wondering when backup troops would arrive to help them.

Through the thick smoke and debris, Baker saw a German soldier waving a white flag with a red cross, followed by a platoon carrying stretchers.

"We've got to shoot them!" Baker's men whispered.

But Baker refused. "Hold your fire. If we shoot their medics, then they'll shoot ours."

When the Germans were 50 yards away, they dropped their

stretchers and whipped off the blankets, revealing hidden machine guns. "We've been tricked!" As the Germans picked up their weapons, Baker yelled, "Fire!" The Americans cut loose with a vengeance, mowing down the fake medics until the rest of the Germans ran off.

By now, Baker and his exhausted, dirty, blood-caked men were nearly out of ammunition. As the dust cleared, so did his thinking. *We have too little ammo to attack the castle, and it's pretty obvious that no reinforcements are coming. There never were going to be any. The captain was going to let us die out here. We came so close, but it's no use now, not with so few men and little ammo.* Baker sighed and said, "Men, it's time to withdraw."

As his battered troops retreated, Baker remained behind to cover them, picking off one German and sending three others fleeing into the brush. Mortar fire started raining down again as the men raced down the hill. One of the soldiers fell dead, and Baker stopped long enough to jerk the dog tags from his neck. As the rest fled, they were met by sniper fire until one of Baker's men, Sergeant James Thomas, shot the German out of the tree.

But then the soldiers were pinned down by the rapid fire below them from two machine-gun nests that they had missed seeing on their way up the hill. The nests had to be destroyed if the men were to escape. "I'll take them out," said Baker. "Thomas, cover me." Thomas ripped off a flurry of rounds as Baker, low-crawling while cradling his M-1 in his elbows, snaked his way toward the back of the nearest nest. Thomas's bullets flew over Baker's head. *My luck had better not run out now,* Baker thought, *or I'll get my rear shot off by friendly fire.*

When he reached the back entrance of the nest, he lay on his side, pulled out a grenade, and lobbed it inside. He rolled away seconds before the nest exploded, sending dirt and splintered wood flying into the air. *One down and one to go.*

After he signaled Thomas to start another firefight, this time with the Germans in the other nest, Baker sneaked up on the enemy from behind. In exactly the same way as before, he blew up the nest, silencing its machine gun. Then he got up and covered his men as they sprinted down the hill through the brush and back to the main road at the bottom, where American trucks, tanks, jeeps, and troops were gathering.

Of the 26 men in his platoon, only seven returned. Baker and his brave men had been fighting for 12 straight hours. He had wiped out six machine-gun nests, two observation posts, and killed more than a dozen Germans. He finally caught his breath. And then he threw up.

Baker had seen violent death before, but this was different. He couldn't get rid of the images in his mind of the men in his platoon who had been blown to pieces. He had fought side by side with them, laughed with them, eaten with them, and written letters for them. Now 19 of them were dead. When he reached headquarters, he pulled out of his pockets the bloodstained dog tags he had collected and dropped them on the company clerk's desk. *I hate war.*

He looked down and noticed a piece of shrapnel had lodged in the metal case of the compass that he kept on the right side of his webbing belt. If the shrapnel hadn't been deflected by the compass, it would have sliced into his groin and severed an artery, causing him to bleed to death. His eyes watered up. *Why was I so lucky, and nineteen of my men weren't?*

His sadness turned to anger when he learned what the captain said upon returning to headquarters. The captain had told the battalion commander not to worry about the black troops, because they had been wiped out. Baker seethed. *They had no intention of sending us help. They left us out there to die.*

Baker was summoned to the office of Colonel Raymond Sherman, who headed the regiment. *What are the chances that I'll hear one word of appreciation for the sacrifices of my men?* Baker wondered. *Slim to none.* He was right. Racism trumped respect. Rather than offer Baker solace for his slaughtered platoon or praise him for his courageous actions, the colonel chewed him out for not wearing his helmet in battle and setting a bad example for his men.

Then the colonel told him, "The Four hundred seventy-third is taking over the advance tomorrow, and they need somebody who knows the terrain. You're volunteering to lead them. Now get out of here and wear your helmet tomorrow, or I'll bust you to buck private!"

The next day, Baker led the all-white company up the hill, where they were met with little resistance. By then, most of the Germans had fled. Thanks to the gutsy efforts of Baker and his men, the western edge of the Gothic Line finally had been breached.

"We proved we could go up and fight and die," he told the surviving members of his platoon. "We had cleared the way and made liars out of everyone who said we couldn't do it." He felt good about that. But he was angry that he and the black soldiers had yet to receive the respect and acknowledgment they deserved from the top brass.

Despite the racism, Baker was promoted to first lieutenant several weeks later. He also was awarded the Purple Heart and the Distinguished Service Cross, making him one of the most decorated black soldiers in the war. But what he really wanted — admission from the white commanders that the black soldiers had fought valiantly — he never received.

Nevertheless, Baker remained in the Army after the war and lived through its desegregation, becoming one of the first blacks to command an all-white company. After retiring from the Army, he spent nearly 20 years working for the Red Cross. The anger he felt for the way he and his fellow blacks were treated slowly diminished with time.

He came to accept the fact that of the 433 Medals of Honor given to soldiers who fought during World War II, not one was awarded to an African-American, even though there were 1.7 million black troops.

But then a study commissioned by the U.S. Army in the 1990s concluded that racial discrimination among white commanders hid the truth about the combat heroics of African-Americans. Investigators examined battle records and interviewed former soldiers and concluded that seven blacks deserved the Medal of Honor. One of them was Vernon Baker.

He was stunned when he heard the news. It didn't seem possible that more than half a century after he had led that bold charge toward Castle Aghinolfi, Baker was finally getting the recognition that he and his platoon deserved. At a ceremony at the White House in 1997, President Bill Clinton awarded Medals of Honor to Baker and six other black soldiers. Baker, 76 at the time, was the only recipient still living.

Accepting the honor, Baker broke down in tears. He didn't cry for himself but for all the heroes who died on Hill X that fateful day in April 1945. "We knew we were fighting for a country that didn't appreciate us, and yet we were proud to fight," Baker said. "President Clinton said we Medal of Honor recipients 'were denied the nation's highest honor, but their deeds could not be denied.' Those words describe my platoon and all of the black men who have valiantly gone to combat in every war this country has ever fought."

After his retirement, Baker moved with his wife, Heidy, into a cabin in northern Idaho. He wrote a book about his life called Lasting Valor, *which supplied some of the material for this story.*

About the Author

Allan Zullo is the author of more than 90 nonfiction books on subjects ranging from sports and the supernatural to history and animals.

He has written the bestselling Haunted Kids series, published by Scholastic, filled with chilling stories based on, or inspired by, documented cases from the files of ghost hunters. Allan also has introduced Scholastic readers to the Ten True Tales series, about people who have met the challenges of dangerous, sometimes life-threatening, situations. In addition, he has authored two books about the real-life experiences of kids during the Holocaust — *Survivors: True Stories of Children in the Holocaust* and *Heroes of the Holocaust: True Stories of Rescues by Teens*.

Allan, the grandfather of three boys and the father of two grown daughters, lives with his wife on the side of a mountain near Asheville, North Carolina. To learn more about the author, visit his Web site at www.allanzullo.com.